Provinces
and
Provincial Capitals
of the World

compiled by

Morris Fisher

The Scarecrow Press, Inc.
New York   1967

Table of Contents

iv

Arrangement

The listing presents:

1. the popular or common name for the nation discussed

2. the official or formal name for the nation

3. the native name for the nation (if in current use)

4. the national capital city

5. the location of the country according to continent

6. the general description of its major administrative divisions

7. the general description of its minor administrative divisions

8. the specific naming of its major administrative divisions and their seats of administration

9. further notes on the minor administrative divisions

Afghanistan (popular name)

The Kingdom of Afghanistan (official name)

"Doulat I Padsháhí Ye Afghanistan" (native name)

Kabul (national capital)

Afghanistan is in Southern Asia. It is bounded by the U.S.-
S.R. on the north; by China and India on the northeast;
by Pakistan on the south and southeast; and by Iran on
the west.

The Major Administrative Divisions of Afghanistan are the
15 Provinces or "Wilayut."

The minor administrative divsisions are called districts and
subdistricts.

Provinces:	Provincial Capitals:
1. Herát	Herát
2. Kabul	Kabul
3. Mazár-i-Sharif	Mazár-i-Sharif
4. Nangarhar	Jalalabad
5. Paktya	Gardez
6. Kandahár	Kandahár
7. Kataghan	Baghlan
8. Badakhshán	Faizabad
9. Faráh	Faráh
10. Ghazni	Ghazni
11. Girishk	Girishk
12. Maimana	Maimana
13. Shibarghan	Shibarghan
14. Parwan	Charikar
15. Ghore	Ghore

Albania (popular name)

The People's Republic of Albania (official name)

"Republika Popullóre e Shqipërïsë" (native name)

Albania (continued)

Tirana (national capital)

Albania is located in Southeastern Europe.

Albania is bounded by the Adriatic Sea on the west; by Yugoslavia on the north and northeast; and by Greece on the
southeast and south.

The Major Administrative Divisions of Albania are the 10
Prefectures.

The minor administrative divisions of Albania are called districts or "rrethe;" and the subdistricts are called "loka-
litete" and "fshatra."

Prefectures:	Prefectural Capitals:
1. Berat	Berat
2. Dibër	Dibër
3. Durrës	Durrës
4. Elbasan	Elbasan
5. Gjinokastër	Gjinokastër
6. Korçë	Korçë
7. Shkodër	Shkodër
8. Vlonë	Vlonë
9. Kukës	Kukës
10. Tirana	Tirana

Algeria (popular name)

The Democratic and Popular Republic of Algeria

"Algerie" (native name)

Algiers (national capital)

Algeria is located in Northern Africa. It is bounded by the
Mediterranean Sea on the north; by Morocco and Spanish
West Africa on the west; by Tunisia and Libya on the
east; and by Mauritania, Mali, and Niger on the south.

The Major Administrative Divisions of Algeria are the 15
"Départements."

The minor administrative divisions of Algeria are the 81
"arrondissements" and the 681 "communes."

"Départements:"	Capitals of "Départements:"
1. Tizi-Ouzou	Tizi-Ouzou
2. Orléansville	Orléansville
3. Medea	Medea
4. Oran	Oran
5. Tlemcen	Tlemcen
6. Mostaganem	Mostagenem
7. Tiaret	Tiaret
8. Constantine	Constantine
9. Bône	Bône
10. Sétif	Sétif
11. Batna	Batna
12. Algiers	Algiers
13. Saida	Saida
14. Oasis	Quargla
15. Saoura	Comb-Béchar

Andorra (popular name)

The Republic of Andorra (official name)

"Valls D'Andorra" (native name)

Andorra-La-Vella (national capital)

Andorra is located in Southwestern Europe. It is bounded
by France on the north and northeast; and by Spain on the
southeast, south, and west.

The Major Administrative Districts of Andorra are the 6
Districts.

The minor administrative districts of Andorra are the communes or "comuns" and the "corts."

Districts:	District Capitals:
1. Canillo	Canillo
2. Encamps	Encamps
3. Ordino	Ordino
4. Massana	Massana
5. Sant Julia de Loria	Sant Julia de Loria
6. Andorra-La-Vella	Andorra-La-Vella

Argentina (popular name)

The Argentine Republic (official name)

"República Argentina" (native name)

Argentina (continued)

Buenos Aires (national capital)

Argentina is located in Southeastern South America. It is
bounded by Bolivia and Paraguay on the north; by Brazil
and Uruguay on the northeast; by the Atlantic Ocean on
the southeast, and by Chile on the west and south.

The Major Administrative Divisions of Argentina number 24:
the 22 Provinces, the 1 national territory, and the 1
Federal District.

Major Administrative Div.	Capitals of Major Adm. Div.
1. Buenos Aires Province	La Plata
2. Catamarca Province	Catamarca
3. Cordoba Province	Cordoba
4. Corrientes Province	Corrientes
5. Chaco Province	Resistencia
6. Chubut Province	Rawson
7. Entre Rios Province	Parana
8. Formosa Province	Formosa
9. Jujuy Province	Jujuy
10. La Pampa Province	Santa Rosa
11. La Rioja Province	La Rioja
12. Mendoza Province	Mendoza
13. Misiones Province	Posadas
14. Neuquen Province	Neuquen
15. Rio Negro Province	Viedma
16. Salta Province	Salta
17. San Juan Province	San Juan
18. San Luis Province	San Luis
19. Santa Cruz Province	Rio Gallegos
20. Santa Fe Province	Santa Fe
21. Santiago del Estero Prov.	Santiago del Estero
22. Tucuman Province	Tucuman
23. Tierra del Fuego Nat. Territory	Ushuaia
24. Distrito Federal	Buenos Aires

Australia (popular name)

The Commonwealth of Australia (official name)

Canberra (national capital)

Australia is located and co-extensive with the Australian
continent, southeast of Mainland Asia. It is an island
bounded by the Indian Ocean on the west and south; and
by the Pacific Ocean and the Timor Sea on the east and
north.

The Major Administrative Divisions of Australia number 16:
the 6 States; the 2 Mainland Territories; and the 8 External Territories.

The minor administrative divisions comprise counties, districts, shires, boroughs, municipalities, commissions,
cities, and towns.

Major Administrative Div.	Capitals of Major Adm. Div.
1. New South Wales State	Sydney
2. Queensland State	Brisbane
3. South Australia State	Adelaide
4. Tasmania State	Hobart
5. Victoria State	Melbourne
6. Western Australia State	Perth
7. Australian Capital Terri- tory (mainland)	Canberra
8. Northern Territory (main- land)	Darwin
9. Ashmore and Cartier Is. Territory	(uninhabited)
10. Christmas Island Terr.	Christmas Is.
11. Cocos Islands Terr.	Home Island
12. McDonald and Heard Is. Territory	(uninhabited)
13. Norfolk Island Territory	Kingston
14. Nauru Trust Territory	Nauru
15. Australian Antarctic Terr.	Mawson
16. Papua and New Guinea Territory	Port Moresby

Further notes on territorial subdivisions:

New South Wales State is divided into 39 county councils, 131
shires, and 107 municipalities.

Queensland State is divided into 112 shires, 12 cities, and 10
towns.

South Australia State is divided into 49 counties, 21 cities, 22
country corporations, and 100 district councils.

Australia (continued)

Tasmania State is divided into 45 municipalities; 2 commissions, and 2 cities.

Victoria State is divided into 137 shires, 42 cities, 4 towns, and 18 boroughs.

Western Australia State is divided into 126 shires, 15 towns, and 5 cities.

The Territory of Papua and New Guinea is divided into 16 districts, 41 sub-districts, and 88 local government councils. The districts are:

Districts	District Capitals
1. Western Highlands	Wabag
2. Morobe	Lae
3. Eastern Highlands	Goroka
4. Northern	Kokoda
5. Milne Bay	Samarai
6. West Central	Kairuku
7. Manus	Lorengau
8. New Ireland	Kavieng
9. Bougainville	Sohano
10. New Britain	Rabaul
11. Madang	Madang
12. Sepik	Wewak
13. Southern Highlands	Mendi
14. Gulf	Kerema
15. Western	Daru
16. East Central	Port Moresby

Austria (popular name)

The Federal Republic of Austria (official name)

"Republik Österreich" (native name)

Vienna (national capital)

Austria is located in Central Europe.

Austria is bounded by Switzerland and Liechtenstein on the west; by Germany and Czechoslovakia on the north; by Hungary on the east; and by Italy and Yugoslavia on the south.

14

The Major Administrative Divisions of Austria are the 9 Provinces or "länder."

The minor administrative divisions of Austria are the districts or "bezirken," and the communes.

Provinces	Provincial Capitals
1. Burgenland	Eisenstadt
2. Kärnten	Klagenfurt
3. Niederösterreich	Wien
4. Oberösterreich	Linz
5. Salzburg	Salzburg
6. Steiermark	Graz
7. Tirol	Innsbruck
8. Vorarlberg	Bregenz
9. Wien	Wien

Bahrain (popular name)

The Sheikhdom of Bahrain (official name)

Manama (national capital)

Bahrain is located in Southwestern Asia, off of Arabia's eastern coast, halfway down the Persian Gulf. It is an island sheikhdom bounded by Qatar to the east; by Saudi Arabia to the south and west; and by the Persian Gulf on the north.

Bahrain's administrative divisions comprise its 4 municipalities:

1. Manama
2. Muharraq
3. Hedd
4. Rifaa

Belgium (popular name)

The Kingdom of Belgium (official name)

"Royaume de Belgique" (native name)

Brussels (national capital)

Belgium is located in Northwestern Europe. It is bounded by the North Sea on the west; by the Netherlands on the north; by Germany and Luxembourg on the east; and by France on the south.

Belgium (continued)

The Major Administrative Divisions of Belgium are the 9
Provinces.

The minor administrative divisions of Belgium are the "arrondissements" and the "communes."

Provinces	Provincial Capitals
1. Antwerpen	Antwerpen (Antwerp)
2. Brabant	Brussels
3. Hainaut	Mons
4. Liège	Liège
5. Limburg	Hasselt
6. Luxembourg	Arlon
7. Namur	Namur
8. Oost-Vlaanderen	Ghent
9. West-Vlaanderen	Bruges

Bhutan (popular name)

The Kingdom of Bhutan (official name)

"Druk-Yul" (native name)

Thimbu (national capital)

Bhutan is located in Southern Asia. It is bounded by Tibet
on the north; by India on the east and south; and by Sikkim on the west.

The Major Administrative Divisions of Bhutan are the 9
Provinces or "penlop."

The minor administrative divisions are called districts.

Provinces	Provincial Capitals
1. Paro	Paro Dzong
2. Thimbu	Tashi Chho Dzong
3. Tagana	Taga Dzong
4. Punakha	Punakha
5. Wangü-Phodrang	Wangü-Phodrang
6. Tongsa	Tongsa Dzong
7. Byakar	Byakar
8. Ha	Ha
9. Dukye	Dukye

Bolivia (popular name)

The Republic of Bolivia (official name)

"República de Bolivia" (native name)

La Paz (national capital)

Bolivia is located in West-central South America. It is
bounded by Brazil on the north and east; by Paraguay on
the southeast; by Argentina on the south; and by Chile
and Peru on the west.

The Major Administrative Divisions of Bolivia are the 9 Departments.

The minor administrative divisions of Bolivia are the 87
provinces and the 940 cantons.

Departments	Capitals of Departments
1. La Paz	La Paz
2. Cochabamba	Cochabamba
3. Potasi	Potasi
4. Santa Cruz	Santa Cruz
5. Chuquisaca	Sucre
6. Tarija	Tarija
7. Oruro	Oruro
8. Beni	Trinidad
9. Pando	Cobija

Brazil (popular name)

The United States of Brazil (official name)

"Estados Unidos do Brasil" (native name)

Brasilia (national capital)

Brazil is located in Central and Eastern South America, the
largest nation on that continent. It is bounded by Venezuela, Surinam, British Guiana, and French Guiana on
the north; by the Atlantic Ocean on the east; by Uruguay,
Argentina, and Paraguay on the south; and by Bolivia,
Peru, and Colombia on the west.

The Major Administrative Divisions of Brazil number 28:
the 22 States or "estados;"

17

Brazil (continued)

the 4 Territories or "territorios;"
the 1 Federal District or "districto federal;" and
the 1 "Zona Litigiosa" or
area of unsettled jurisdiction.

The minor administrative divisions of Brazil are the districts and municipalities.

Major Administrative Div.	Capitals of Major Adm. Div.
1. Alagôas State	Maceió
2. Bahia State	Salvador
3. Ceará State	Fortaleza
4. Espírito Santo State	Espérito Santo
5. Goiás State	Goiania
6. Maranhaó State	Maranhaó
7. Matto Grosso State	Matto Grasso
8. Minas Gerais State	Belo Horizonte
9. Pará State	Belem
10. Paraíba State	Paraíba
11. Pernambuco State	Recife
12. Paraná State	Curitiba
13. Rio de Janeiro State	Niteroi
14. Rio Grande Do Norte State	Rio Grande Do Norte
15. Rio Grande Do Sul State	Porto Alegre
16. Santa Catarina State	Santa Catarina
17. Piauí State	Piauí
18. São Paulo State	São Paulo
19. Sergipe State	Sergipe
20. Amazonas State	Manaus
21. Acre State	Acre
22. Guanabara State	Rio de Janeiro
23. Roraima Territory	Boa Vista
24. Rondônia Territory	Pôrto Velho
25. Amapá Territory	Macapá
26. Fernando de Noronha Territory	Fernando de Noronha
27. "Distrito Federal"	Brasilia
28. "Zona Litigiosa"	

Brunei (popular name)

The Sultanate of Brunei (official name)

Brunei Town (national capital)

Brunei is located in Southeast Asia, on the north side of the

18

East Indies island of Borneo. It is bounded by the South China Sea on the west and north; and by the Malaysian State of Sarawak on the east and south.

Brunei's administrative divisions are its 4 district councils.

Districts	District Capitals
1. Brunei And Muara	Brunei Town
2. Belait	Belait
3. Tutong	Tutong
4. Temburong	Temburong

Bulgaria (popular name)

The People's Republic of Bulgaria (official name)

"Narodna Republika Bulgaria" (native name)

Sofia (national capital)

Bulgaria is located in Southeastern Europe. It is bounded by Rumania on the north; by Yugoslavia on the west; by Greece on the south; by Turkey on the southeast; and by the Black Sea on the east.

The Major Administrative Divisions of Bulgaria are the 30 Provinces or "okrugs."

The minor administrative divisions of Bulgaria are the 1012 communes or "obshtina."

Provinces	Provincial Capitals
1. Vidin	Vidin
2. Mihailovgrad	Mihailovgrad
3. Pleven	Pleven
4. Vratsa	Vratsa
5. Dimitrovo	Dimitrovo
6. Kyustendil	Kyustendil
7. Blagoevgrad	Blagoevgrad
8. Smolyan	Smolyan
9. Kurdjali	Kurdjali
10. Plovdiv	Plovdiv
11. Plovdiv City	Provdiv City
12. Pazardjik	Pazardjik
13. Stara Zagora	Stara Zagora
14. Lovech	Lovech
15. Turnovo	Turnovo

19

Bulgaria (continued)

16.	Gabrovo	Gabrovo
17.	Yambol	Yambol
18.	Sliven	Sliven
19.	Kousso	Kousso
20.	Razrad	Razrad
21.	Silistra	Silistra
22.	Tolbukhin	Tolbukhin
23.	Varna	Varna
24.	Varna City	Varna City
25.	Kolarovgrad	Kolarovgrad
26.	Bourgas	Bourgas
27.	Torgovishte	Torgovishte
28.	Sofia City	Sofia City
29.	Haskovo	Haskovo
30.	Ruse	Ruse

Burma (popular name)

The Union of Burma (official name)

"Pyee-Daung-Su Myanma-Nainggan-Daw" (native name)

Rangoon (national capital)

Burma is located in Southeastern Asia. It is bounded by China on the north; by China, Laos and Thailand on the east; by the Bay of Bengal on the south; and by India, Pakistan, and the Bay of Bengal on the west.

The Major Administrative Divisions of Burma number 12:
the 7 Burma Proper administrative divisions;
the 4 States, and
the 1 Special Division

The minor administrative divisions of Burma are called districts.

Major Administrative Div.	Capitals of Major Adm. Div.
1. Arakan Division	Akyub
2. Pegu Division	Rangoon
3. Irrawaddy Division	Bassein
4. Tenasserim Division	Moulmein
5. Magwe Division	Magwe
6. Mandalay Division	Mandalay
7. Sagaing Division	Sagaing

8.	Kachin State	Myitkyina
9.	Shan State	Taunggyi
10.	Kayah State	Loi-kaw
11.	Karen State	Pa-an
12.	Chin Hills Special Div.	Falam

Burundi (popular name)

The Kingdom of Burundi (official name)

"Royaume du Burundi" (native name)

Bujumbura (national capital)

Burundi is located in East-Central Africa. It is bounded by
Rwanda on the north; by Tanzania on the east and south;
and by Congo (Léopoldville) on the west.

The Major Administrative Divisions of Burundi are the 9
Provinces.

The minor administrative divisions of Burundi are the 5
"arrondissements" and the 181 "communes."

Provinces	Provincial Capitals
1. Bujumbura	Bujumbura
2. Kitega	Kitega
3. Bubanza	Bubanza
4. Muramvya	Muramvya
5. Ngozi	Ngozi
6. Muhinga	Muhinga
7. Ruyigi	Ruyigi
8. Bururi	Bururi
9. Rutana	Rutana

Cambodia (popular name)

The Kingdom of Cambodia (official name)

"Royaume de Cambodge" (native name)

Phnom Penh (national capital)

Cambodia is located in Southeast Asia. It is bounded by
Laos and Thailand on the north; by Thailand on the west;
by the Gulf of Siam on the south; and by South Vietnam
on the east.

Cambodia (continued)

The Major Administrative Divisions of Cambodia are the 18 Provinces or "khet."

The minor administrative divisions are the districts or "srok."

Provinces	Provincial Capitals
1. Kandal	Kandal
2. Takeo	Takeo
3. Kampot	Kampot
4. Kompong Speu	Kompong Speu
5. Koh Kong	Koh Kong
6. Kompong Chhnang	Kompong Chhnang
7. Pursat	Pursat
8. Battambang	Battambang
9. Siem Reap	Siem Reap
10. Kompong Thom	Kompong Thom
11. Stung Treng	Stung Treng
12. Ratanakiri	Andaung Pich
13. Kratie	Kratie
14. Kompong Cham	Kompong Cham
15. Prey Veng	Prey Veng
16. Svay Rieng	Svay Rieng
17. Mondolkiri	Mondolkiri
18. Phnom Penh (Capital City)	

Cameroon (popular name)

The Federal Republic of Cameroon (official name)

"La République Féderale du Cameroon" (native name)

Yaoundé (national capital)

Cameroon is located in Western Africa. It is bounded by Nigeria on the north and northwest; by Chad on the northeast; by the Central African Republic on the east; and by Congo (Brazzaville), Gabon, and Spanish Rio Muni on the south.

The Major Administrative Divisions of Cameroon are the 33 "Départements."

The minor administrative divisions of Cameroon are the 22 districts and the 93 "arrondissements."

"Départements"	Capitals of "Départements"
1. Dja et Lobo	Sangmélima
2. Ntem	Ebolowa
3. Kribi	Kribi
4. Haut Nyong	Abong Mbang
5. Boumba Ngoko	Yokadouma
6. Nyong et Kélé	Eséka
7. Sanaga Maritîme	Edea
8. Nyong et So	Mbalmayo
9. Likie	Obala
10. Nyong et Mfoumou	Akonolinga
11. Wouri	Douala
12. Victoria	Victoria
13. Kumba	Kumba
14. Mungo	Nkongsamba
15. Mefou	Yaoundé
16. Nkam	Yabassi
17. Ndé	Bangangté
18. Haute Nkam	Bafang
19. Menoua	Dschang
20. Bamboutos	Mbouda
21. Mamfe	Mamfe
22. Nkambe	Nkambe
23. Bamenda	Bamenda
24. Bamoun	Foumban
25. Wum	Wum
26. Haute Sanaga	Nanga-Eboko
27. Lom et Kadei	Batouri
28. Adamoua	Ngaoundéré
29. Bénoué	Garoua
30. Diamaré	Maroua
31. Margui-Wandala	Mokolo
32. Mayo-Danai	Yagoua
33. Logone et Chari	Fort-Foureau

Canada (popular name)

The Dominion of Canada (official name)

Ottawa (national capital)

Canada is located in Northern North America. It is bounded
by the Baffin Bay, the Gulf of St. Lawrence, and the Atlantic Ocean on the east; by the Atlantic Ocean and the
United States on the south; by the Pacific Ocean and
Alaska on the west; and by the Arctic Ocean on the north.

Canada (continued)

The Major Administrative Divisions of Canada number 12: the 10 Provinces and the 2 Territories.

The minor administrative divisions of Canada include counties, towns, municipalities, districts, and cities.

Major Administrative Div.	Capitals of Major Adm. Div.
1. Alberta Province	Edmonton
2. British Columbia Province	Victoria
3. Manitoba Province	Winnipeg
4. New Brunswick Province	Fredericton
5. Newfoundland Province	St. Johns'
6. Nova Scotia Province	Halifax
7. Ontario Province	Toronto
8. Prince Edward Is. Province	Charlottetown
9. Quebec Province	Quebec City
10. Saskatchewan Province	Regina
11. Northwest Territories	Ontario
12. Yukon Territory	Whitehorse

Further notes on Canada's minor divisions:

Alberta is divided into 20 counties and 277 municipalities.

British Columbia is divided into 32 cities, 30 districts, 4 towns, 59 villages, and 2 local districts.

Manitoba has 17 local government districts, 110 rural municipalities and 71 urban municipalities.

New Brunswick has 15 counties and 27 incorporated municipalities.

Newfoundland has 49 incorporated towns, 4 rural district councils, 2 cities, 50 community councils, and 7 local improvement districts.

Nova Scotia has 18 geographical counties, 39 towns, 3 cities, and 24 municipalities.

Ontario has 43 municipal counties and 11 northern districts.

Prince Edward Island has 3 counties.

Quebec has 74 county corporations, 2 city corporations, and 1671 municipalities.

24

Saskatchewan has 529 rural municipalities, 11 cities, 116 town, and 356 villages.

The Northwest Territory is divided into 3 districts: Mackenzie, Keewatin, and Franklin.

The Yukon Territory is divided into 7 Electoral districts: Dawson, Whitehorse-East, Whitehorse-North, Whitehorse-West, Carmachs-Kluane, Mayo, and Watson Lake.

Central African Republic (popular and official name)

"La République Centrafricaine" (native name)

Bangui (national capital)

The Central African Republic is located in Central Africa. It is bounded by Chad on the north; by Sudan on the east; by Congo (Léopoldville) and Congo (Brazzaville) on the south; and by Cameroon on the west.

The Major Administrative Divisions of the Central African Republic number 50: the 14 Prefectures and the 36 Sub-Prefectures.

Major Administrative Div.	Capitals of Major Adm. Div.
1. Ombella-M'Poko Prefecture	Bangui
2. Birao Prefecture	Birao
3. Buar-Baboua Prefecture	Bouar
4. Kémo-Gribingui Prefecture	Fort-Sibut
5. Basse-Kotto Prefecture	Mobaye
6. Haute-Kotto Prefecture	Bria
7. Lobaye Prefecture	M'Baiki
8. M'Bomou Prefecture	Bangassou
9. N'Dele Prefecture	N'Dele
10. Obo-Zemio Prefecture	Obo
11. Ouaka Prefecture	Bambari
12. Ouham Prefecture	Bassangoa
13. Ouham-Pendé Prefecture	Bozoum
14. Haute-Sangha Prefecture	Berbérati
15. Bimbo Sub-Prefecture	Bimbo
16. Bossembélé Sub-Prefecture	Bossembélé
17. Damara Sub-Prefecture	Damara
18. Baboua Sub-Prefecture	Baboua
19. Fort-Sibut Sub-Prefecture	Fort-Sibut
20. Dekoa Sub-Prefecture	Dekoa
21. Fort-Crampel Sub-Prefecture	Fort-Crampel

Canada (continued)

22.	Mobaye Sub-Prefecture	Mobaye
23.	Alindao Sub-Prefecture	Alindao
24.	Kembé Sub-Prefecture	Kembé
25.	Bria Sub-Prefecture	Bria
26.	Yalinga Sub-Prefecture	Yalinga
27.	Ouadda Sub-Prefecture	Ouadda
28.	M'Baiki Sub-Prefecture	M'Baiki
29.	Boda Sub-Prefecture	Boda
30.	Mongoumba Sub-Prefecture	Mongoumba
31.	Bangassou Sub-Prefecture	Bangassou
32.	Bakouma Sub-Prefecture	Bakouma
33.	Ouango Sub-Prefecture	Ouango
34.	Rafai Sub-Prefecture	Rafai
35.	Obo Sub-Prefecture	Obo
36.	Zemio Sub-Prefecture	Zemio
37.	Bambari Sub-Prefecture	Bambari
38.	Bakala Sub-Prefecture	Bakala
39.	Grimari Sub-Prefecture	Grimari
40.	Ippy Sub-Prefecture	Ippy
41.	Kouango Sub-Prefecture	Kouango
42.	Bassangoa Sub-Prefecture	Bassangoa
43.	Batangafo Sub-Prefecture	Batangafo
44.	Bouca Sub-Prefecture	Bouca
45.	Bozoum Sub-Prefecture	Bozoum
46.	Bocaranga Sub-Prefecture	Bocaranga
47.	Paoua Sub-Prefecture	Paoua
48.	Berlarati Sub-Prefecture	Berlarati
49.	Carnot Sub-Prefecture	Carnot
50.	Nola Sub-Prefecture	Nola

Ceylon (popular name)

The Dominion of Ceylon (official name)

"Sri Lanka" (native name)

Colombo (national capital)

Ceylon is located in Southern Asia. It is an island nation, lying in the Indian Ocean off of India's southern tip.

The Major Administrative Divisions of Ceylon number 30: the 9 Provinces and the 21 Administrative Districts.

The minor administrative divisions of Ceylon comprise 37

26

urban councils, 26 town councils, and 6 municipalities.

Major Administrative Div.	Capitals of Major Adm. Div.
1. Western Province	Colombo
2. Central Province	Kandy
3. Southern Province	Galle
4. Northern Province	Jaffna
5. Eastern Province	Trincomalee
6. Northwestern Province	Kurunegala
7. North Central Province	Anuradhapura
8. Uva Province	Badulla
9. Sabaragamuwa Province	Ratnapura

Districts	District Capitals
1. Colombo	Colombo
2. Kalutara	Kalutara
3. Kandy	Kandy
4. Matale	Matale
5. N'Eliya	N'Eliya
6. Galle	Galle
7. Matara	Matara
8. Hambantota	Hambantota
9. Iaffna	Jaffna
10. Mannar	Mannar
11. Vavaniya	Vavaniya
12. Trincomalee	Trincomalee
13. Batticaloa	Batticaloa
14. Kurunegala	Kurunegala
15. Puttalam	Puttalam
16. Anuradhapura	Anuradhapura
17. Polonaruwa	Polonaruwa
18. Badulla	Badulla
19. Ratnapura	Ratnapura
20. Kegalle	Kegalle
21. Monaragala	Monaragala

Chad (popular name)

The Republic of Chad (official name)

"République du Tchad" (native name)

Fort-Lamy (national capital)

Chad is located in North-central Africa. It is bounded by
Libya on the north; by Sudan on the east; by the Central
African Republic on the south; and by Cameroon, Nigeria,
and Niger on the west.

27

Chad (continued)

The Major Administrative Divisions of Chad number 53: the 11 "Régions" and the 42 Districts.

Major Administrative Div.	Capitals of Major Adm. Div.
1. Chari-Baguirmi Region	Fort-Lamy
2. Mayo-Kebbi Region	Bongor
3. Logone Region	Moundou
4. Moyen-Chari Region	Fort-Archambault
5. Salamat Region	Am-Timan
6. Kanem Region	Mao
7. Batha Region	Ati
8. Ouaddai Region	Abèché
9. Biltine Region	Biltine
10. Bourkou-Ennedi-Tibesti Reg.	Faya-Largeau
11. Guera Region	Mongo
12. Fort-Lamy-Rural District	Fort-Lamy
13. Fort-Lamy Bureau Urbain Dis.	Fort-Lamy
14. Bokoro District	Bokoro
15. Bousso District	Bousso
16. Massakory District	Massakory
17. Massenya District	Massenya
18. Bongor District	Bongor
19. Fianga District	Fianga
20. Lère District	Lère
21. Pala District	Pala
22. Moundou Centre Urbain Dis.	Moundou
23. Moundou District	Moundou
24. Baibokoum District	Baibokoum
25. Doba District	Doba
26. Kelo District	Kelo
27. Lai District	Lai
28. Fort-Archambault Centre Urbain Dist.	Fort-Archambault
29. Fort-Archambault District	Fort-Archambault
30. Koumra District	Koumra
31. Kyabe District	Kyabe
32. Moissala District	Moissala
33. Am-Timan District	Am-Timan
34. Aboudeia District	Aboudeia
35. Haraze District	Haraze
36. Mao District	Mao
37. Nord Nokou-Kanem District	Nord Nokou-Kanem
38. Moussoro District	Moussoro
39. Bol District	Bol
40. Ati District	Ati

41.	Dnor District	Dnor
42.	Oum-Hadjer District	Oum-Hadjer
43.	Abèché Centre Urbain Dis.	Abèché
44.	Abèché District	Abèché
45.	Adre District	Adre
46.	Am-Dam District	Am-Dam
47.	Biltine District	Biltine
48.	Goz-Beida District	Goz-Beida
49.	Borkou District	Borkou
50.	Enredi District	Enredi
51.	Tibesti District	Tibesti
52.	Mongo District	Mongo
53.	Melfi District	Melfi

Chile (popular name)

The Republic of Chile (official name)

"Republica de Chile" (native name)

Santiago (national capital)

Chile is located in Southwestern South America. It is
bounded by Peru on the north; by Bolivia and Argentina
on the east; and by the Pacific Ocean on the south and
west.

The Major Administrative Divisions of Chile number 113:
the 25 Provinces and the 88 Departments.

The minor administrative divisions of Chile are the municipal districts or "distritos" and the smaller "subdelagaci-
ones."

Major Administrative Div.		Capitals of Major Adm. Div.
1.	Aconcagua Province	San Felipe
2.	Antofagasta Province	Antofagasta
3.	Arauco Province	Lebu
4.	Atacama Province	Copiapo
5.	Aysén Province	Puerto Aysen
6.	Bio-Bio Province	Los Angeles
7.	Cautín Province	Temuco
8.	Chiloé Province	Ancud
9.	Colchagua Province	San Fernando
10.	Concepción Province	Concepción
11.	Coquimbo Province	La Serena
12.	Curicó Province	Curico
13.	Linares Province	Linares

Chile (continued)

14. Llanquihue Province	Puerto Montt
15. Magallanes Province	Punta Arenas
16. Malleco Province	Angol
17. Maule Province	Couquenes
18. Nuble Province	Chillán
19. O'Higgins Province	Rancagua
20. Osorno Province	Osorno
21. Santiago Province	Santiago
22. Talca Province	Talca
23. Tarapaca Province	Iquique
24. Valdivia Province	Valdivia
25. Valparaiso Province	Valparaiso

Note: "Territorio Antártico Chielno" (The Chilean Antarctic Territory) is a dependency of The Province of Magallanes.

26. Arica Department	Arica
27. Pisagua Department	Pisagua
28. Iquique Department	Iquique
29. Tocopilla Department	Tocopilla
30. El Loa Department	El Loa
31. Antofagasta Department	Antofagasta
32. Taltal Department	Taltal
33. Chañaral Department	Chañaral
34. Copiapó Department	Copiapó
35. Huasco Department	Huasco
36. Fririna Department	Fririna
37. La Serena Department	La Serena
38. Elqui Department	Elqui
39. Coquimbo Department	Coquimbo
40. Ovalle Department	Ovalle
41. Combarbalá Department	Combarbalá
42. Illapel Department	Illapel
43. Petorca Department	Petorca
44. San Felipe Department	San Felipe
45. Los Andes Department	Los Andes
46. Quillota Department	Quillota
47. Valparaiso Department	Valparaiso
48. Santiago Department	Santiago
49. Talagante Department	Talagante
50. Melipilla Department	Melipilla
51. San Antonio Department	San Antonio
52. San Bernardo Department	San Bernardo
53. Maipu Department	Maipu
54. Puente Alto Department	Puente Alto

55.	Rancagua Department	Rancagua
56.	Cachapoal Department	Cachapoal
57.	San Vicente Department	San Vicente
58.	Caupolicán Department	Caupolicán
59.	Santa Cruz Department	Santa Cruz
60.	San Fernando Department	San Fernando
61.	Curicó Department	Curicó
62.	Mataquito Department	Mataquito
63.	Talca Department	Talca
64.	Lonteupé Department	Lonteupé
65.	Curepto Department	Curepto
66.	Constitución Department	Constitución
67.	Chanco Department	Chanco
68.	Cauquenes Department	Cauquenes
69.	Loncomilla Department	Loncomilla
70.	Linares Department	Linares
71.	Parral Department	Parral
72.	Itata Department	Itata
73.	San Carlos Department	San Carlos
74.	Chillán Department	Chillán
75.	Bulnes Department	Bulnes
76.	Yungay Department	Yungay
77.	Tomé Department	Tomé
78.	Talcahuano Department	Talcahuano
79.	Concepción Department	Concepción
80.	Coronel Department	Coronel
81.	Yumbel Department	Yumbel
82.	Arauco Department	Arauco
83.	Lebu Department	Lebu
84.	Cañet Department	Cañet
85.	Laja Department	Laja
86.	Nacimiento Department	Nacimiento
87.	Mulchen Department	Mulchen
88.	Mulchen Department	Angol
89.	Collipulli Department	Collipulli
90.	Traiguen Department	Traiguen
91.	Victoria Department	Victoria
92.	Curacautin Department	Curacautin
93.	Lautaro Department	Lautaro
94.	Imperial Department	Imperial
95.	Temuco Department	Temuco
96.	Pitrufquen Department	Pitrufquen
97.	Villarrica Department	Villarrica
98.	Valdivia Department	Valdivia
99.	La Unión Department	La Unión
100.	Rio Bueno Department	Rio Bueno
101.	Osorno Department	Osorno

Chile (continued)

		Capital City
102.	Rio Negro Department	Rio Negro
103.	Puerto Varas Department	Puerto Varas
104.	Maullín Department	Maullín
105.	Llanquichue Department	Llanquichue
106.	Calbuco Department	Calbuco
107.	Ancud Department	Ancud
108.	Castro Department	Castro
109.	Quinchao Department	Quinchao
110.	Aysén Department	Aysén
111.	Ultima Esperanza Department	Ultima Esperanza
112.	Magallanes Department	Magallanes
113.	Tierra Del Fuego Department	Tierra Del Fuego

(China) Mainland China (popular name)

The People's Republic of China (official name)

"Ta Chung-Hua Jen-min Kung-Ho Kuo" (native name)

Peking (national capital)

Mainland China is located in Eastern Asia. It is bounded by
Mongolia and the U.S.S.R. on the north; by the U.S.S.R.,
Korea, the Yellow Sea, and the East China Sea on the
east; by North Vietnam, Burma, India, Bhutan, Sikkim,
Nepal, and Afghanistan on the south; and by the U.S.S.R.
on the west.

The Major Administrative Divisions of Mainland China number 28: the 21 Provinces or "sheng;" the 5 Autonomous
National Regions called "tzu-chich-ch'ü;" and the 2 Centrally-Administered Municipalities called "shih."

The minor administrative divisions of Mainland China are
made up of districts, counties or "hsien," and municipalities or "shih."

Major Administrative Div.		Capital of Major Adm. Div.
1.	Anhwei Province	Hofei
2.	Chekiang Province	Hangchow
3.	Fukein Province	Foochow
4.	Heilungkiang Province	Harbin
5.	Honan Province	Cheng-chou
6.	Hopeh Province	T'ien-ching
7.	Hunan Province	Changsha

8.	Hupeh Province	Wu-ch'ang
9.	Kansu Province	Lanchow
10.	Kiangsi Province	Nanchang
11.	Kiangsu Province	Nanking
12.	Kirin Province	Changchun
13.	Kwangtung Province	Kwang-chou
14.	Kweichow Province	Kweiyang
15.	Liaoning Province	Shenyang
16.	Shansi Province	Taiyuan
17.	Shantung Province	Chi-nan
18.	Shensi Province	Sian
19.	Szechwan Province	Chengtu
20.	Yunnan Province	Kumming
21.	Tsinghai Province	Hsi-ning

22.	Inner Mongolian Autonom. Reg.	Huhehot
23.	Kwangsi-Chuang Autonom. Reg.	Nanning
24.	Sinkiang-Uighur Autonom. Region	Wu-lu-mu-ch'i
25.	Tibetan Autonomous Region	Lhasa
26.	Ningsia-Hui Autonomous Region	Ningsia Yin-ch'uan

27.	Peking Municipality	Peking
28.	Shanghai Municipality	Shanghai

(China) Nationalist China (popular name)

The Republic of China (official name)

"Chung-Hua Min-Kuo" (native name)

Taipeh (national capital)

Nationalist China is an island republic located in eastern Asia. The island is named Taiwan or Formosa. Its boundaries face the Philippines on the south; Japan on the north; the China Sea on the west; and the Pacific Ocean on the east.

The Major Administrative Divisions of Nationalist China number 22; the 16 Counties or "hsien," the 5 Municipalities, and the Quemoy County Special Division.

Major Administrative Div.	Capitals of Major Adm. Div.
1. Taipeh County	Panchiao
2. Ilan County	Ilan
3. Taoyuan County	Taoyuan

Nationalist China (continued)

4.	Hsinchu County	Hsinchu
5.	Miaoli County	Miaoli
6.	Taichung County	Fengyuan
7.	Changhua County	Changhua
8.	Nantou County	Nantou
9.	Yunlin County	Touliu
10.	Chiayi County	Chiayi
11.	Tainan County	Hsinying
12.	Kaohsiung County	Fengshan
13.	Pingtung County	Pingtung
14.	Taitung County	Taitung
15.	Hualien County	Hualien
16.	Penghu County	Makung
17.	Taipei Municipality	Taipei
18.	Keelung Municipality	Keelung
19.	Taichung Municipality	Taichung
20.	Tainan Municipality	Tainan
21.	Kaohsiung Municipality	Kaohsiung
22.	Quemoy County Spec. Div.	Quemoy

Colombia (popular name)

The Republic of Colombia (official name)

"La Republica de Colombia" (native name)

Bogota (national capital)

Colombia is located in Northwestern South America. It is
bounded by the Caribbean Sea on the north; by Venezuela
and Brazil on the east; by Ecuador and Peru on the
south; and by the Pacific Ocean on the west.

The Major Administrative Divisions of Colombia number 26:
the 17 Departments, the 4 Intendancies, and the 5 Com-
missaries.

Major Administrative Div.		Capitals of Major Adm. Div.
1.	Antioquia Department	Medellin
2.	Atlántico Department	Barranquillo
3.	Bolívar Department	Cartagena
4.	Boyacá Department	Tunja
5.	Caldas Department	Manizales
6.	Cauca Department	Popayán
7.	Chocó Department	Quibdó

34

8.	Cordoba Department	Monteria
9.	Cundinamarca Department	Bogota
10.	Huila Department	Neiva
11.	Magdalena Department	Santa Marta
12.	Nariño Department	Pasto
13.	Norte de Santander Dept.	Cucuta
14.	Santander Department	Bucaramanga
15.	Tolima Department	Ibaque
16.	Valle del Cauca Department	Cali
17.	Meta Department	Villavicencio
18.	Caquetá Intendancy	Florencia
19.	Arauca Intendancy	Arauca
20.	La Guajira Intendancy	Riohacha
21.	San Andrés y Providencia Intend.	San Andrés
22.	Amazonas Commissary	Leticia
23.	Vaupés Commissary	Mitú
24.	Vichada Commissary	Puerto Carreño
25.	Putumayo Commissary	Mocoa
26.	Guainía Commissary	San Felipe

Congo (Brazzaville) (popular name)

The Republic of Congo (Brazzaville) (official name)

"République du Congo (Brazzaville)" (native name)

Brazzaville (national capital)

Congo (Brazzaville) is located in West-Central Africa. It
is bounded by Cameroon and the Central Africal Republic on the north; by Gabon on the northwest; by Congo
(Léopoldville) on the east and southeast; and by the Atlantic Ocean on the southwest.

The Major Administrative Divisions of Congo (Brazzaville)
number 46: the 11 Prefectures and the 35 Sub-Prefectures.

The minor administrative divisions of Congo (Brazzaville)
are the cantons and communes.

Major Administrative Div.	Capitals of Major Adm. Div.
1. Kouilou Prefecture	Pointe-Noire
2. Alima Prefecture	Boundji
3. Bouenza-Louesse Prefecture	Sibiti
4. Lefini Prefecture	Djambala
5. Likouala Prefecture	Impfondo

35

Congo (Brazzaville) (continued)

6.	Likouala-Mossaka Prefecture	Fort-Rousset
7.	Niari Prefecture	Dolisie
8.	Niari-Louesse Prefecture	Mossendjo
9.	Pool Prefecture	Kinkala
10.	Niari-Bouenza Prefecture	Madingou
11.	Sangha Prefecture	Ouesso
12.	Pointe-Noire Sub-Prefecture	Pointe-Noire
13.	Madingo-Kayes Sub-Prefecture	Kayes
14.	M'Vouti Sub-Prefecture	M'Vouti
15.	Boundji Sub-Prefecture	Boundji
16.	Abala Sub-Prefecture	Abala
17.	Ewo Sub-Prefecture	Ewo
18.	Sibiti Sub-Prefecture	Sibiti
19.	Komono Sub-Prefecture	Komono
20.	Zanaga Sub-Prefecture	Zanaga
21.	Djambaba Sub-Prefecture	Djambaba
22.	Gamboma Sub-Prefecture	Gamboma
23.	Lekana Sub-Prefecture	Lekana
24.	Impfondo Sub-Prefecture	Impfondo
25.	Dongou Sub-Prefecture	Dongou
26.	Epena Sub-Prefecture	Epena
27.	Fort-Rousset Sub-Prefecture	Fort-Rousset
28.	Kellé Sub-Prefecture	Kellé
29.	Makoua Sub-Prefecture	Makoua
30.	Mossaka Sub-Prefecture	Mossaka
31.	Dolisie Sub-Prefecture	Dolisie
32.	Kimongo Sub-Prefecture	Kimongo
33.	Loudima Sub-Prefecture	Loudima
34.	Madingou Sub-Prefecture	Madingou
35.	Boko-Songho Sub-Prefecture	Boko-Songho
36.	Mouyondzi Sub-Prefecture	Mouyondzi
37.	Mossendjo Sub-Prefecture	Mossendjo
38.	Divenie Sub-Prefecture	Divenie
39.	Kibangou Sub-Prefecture	Kibangou
40.	Kinkala Sub-Prefecture	Kinkala
41.	Boko Sub-Prefecture	Boko
42.	Kindamba Sub-Prefecture	Kindamba
43.	Mindouli Sub-Prefecture	Mindouli
44.	Ouesso Sub-Prefecture	Ouesso
45.	Sembe Sub-Prefecture	Sembe
46.	Souanke Sub-Prefecture	Souanke

Congo (Léopoldville) (popular name)

The Democratic Republic of the Congo (official name)

'República Démocratique du Congo'' (native name)

Léopoldville (national capital)

Congo (Léopoldville) is located in West-central Africa. It is bounded by The Central African Republic and Sudan on the north; by Sudan, Uganda, Rwandi, Burundi, and Tanzania on the east; by Zambia on the southeast and south; and by Portuguese Angola and Congo (Brazzaville) on the west and southwest.

The Major Administrative Divisions of Congo (Leopoldville) are the 21 Provinces.

The minor administrative divisions of Congo (Léopoldville) are the administrative districts.

Provinces	Provincial Capitals
1. Ubangi	Gemena
2. Uéle	Paulis
3. Kibali-Ituri	Bunia
4. Nord-Kivu	Sake
5. Kivu-Central	Bukavu
6. Maniema	Kindu
7. Haut-Congo	Stanleyville
8. Moyen-Congo	Lisala
9. Cuvette-Central	Coquillatville
10. Mai-Ndombe	Inongo
11. Kwilu	Kikwit
12. Congo-Central	Lisala
13. Kwango	Kenge
14. Unité-Kasaienne	Tshikapa
15. Luluabourg	Luluabourg
16. Sud-Kasai	Bakwanga
17. Lualaba	Koluezi
18. Katanga-Oriental	Elizabethville
19. Nord-Katanga	Albertville
20. Lomani	Kabinda
21. Sankuru	Ladja

Costa Rica (popular name)

The Republic of Costa Rica (official name)

"La Republica de Costa Rica" (native name)

San José (national capital)

Costa Rica (continued)

Costa Rica is located in Southern North America, in the
area called Middle or Central America. It is bounded
by the Caribbean Sea and Panama on the east; and by
the Pacific Ocean on the south and west.

The Major Administrative Divisions of Costa Rica are the
7 Provinces.

The minor administrative divisions of Costa Rica are the
65 cantons and the 326 districts.

Provinces	Provincial Capitals
1. Alajuela	Alajuela
2. Cartago	Cartago
3. Guanacaste	Guanacaste
4. Heredia	Liberia
5. Limón	Limón
6. Puntarenas	Puntarenas
7. San José	San José

Cuba (popular name)

The Republic of Cuba (official name)

"La Republica de Cuba" (native name)

Havana (national capital)

Cuba is located in Southeastern North America, in the West
Indies. It is bounded by the Gulf of Mexico and the
Straight of Florida on the north; by the Atlantic Ocean
on the east; and by the Caribbean Sea on the south and
west.

The Major Administrative Divisions of Cuba are the 6
Provinces or "provincias."

The minor administrative divisions of Cuba are the districts.

Provinces	Provincial Capitals
1. Camagüey	Camagüey
2. La Habana	La Habana (Havana)
3. Las Villas	Santa Clara
4. Matanzas	Matanzas

5. Oriente	Santiago de Cuba
6. Pinar del Río	Pinar del Río

Cyprus (popular name)

The Republic of Cyprus (official name)

"Demokratia Kypron" (native name)

Nicosia (national capital)

Cyprus is located in Western Asia, in the northeast corner of the Mediterranean Sea. It is an island republic which faces Turkey on the north; Syria on the east; Greece on the west; and the Mediterranean Sea on the south.

The Major Administrative Divisions of Cyprus are the 6 Administrative Districts.

Districts	District Capitals
1. Nicosia	Nicosia
2. Limassol	Limassol
3. Famagusta	Famagusta
4. Larnaca	Larnaca
5. Paphos	Paphos
6. Kyrenia	Kyrenia

Czechoslovakia (popular name)

The Czechoslovak Socialist Republic (official name)

"Československa Socialisticka Republika" (native name)

Prague (national capital)

Czechoslovakia is located in East-central Europe. It is bounded by West Germany on the southwest and west; by East Germany on the northwest and north; by the U.S.S.R. on the east; and by Austria and Hungary on the south.

The Major Administrative Divisions of Czechoslovaki are the 11 Administrative Regions or "kraj."

The minor administrative divisions of Czechoslovakia are the districts or "okres" and the local councils.

Czechoslovakia (continued)

Regions	Regional Capitals
1. Hlavnimesto Praha	Praha
2. Stredocesky	Praha
3. Jihocesky	Ceské Budějovica
4. Zapodocesky	Pilsen
5. Severocesky	Usti-nad Labem
6. Vyochodocesky	Hradec Kralové
7. Jihomoravsky	Brno
8. Severomoravsky	Ostrava
9. Zapodoslovensky	Bratislava
10. Stredoslovensky	Banská Bystrica
11. Vyochodoslovensky	Košice

Dahomey (popular name)

The Republic of Dahomey (official name)

'République de Dahomey'' (native name)

Porto-Novo (national capital)

The Republic of Dahomey is located in western Africa. It is bounded by Niger and Upper Volta on the north; by Nigeria on the east; by the Gulf of Guinea on the south; and by Togo on the west.

The Major Administrative Divisions of Dahomey number 35: the 6 ''départements'' and the 29 prefectures.

The minor administrative divisions of Dahomey are the sub-prefectures.

Major Administrative Div.	Capitals of Major Adm. Div.
1. Sud Département	Cotonou
2. Sud-Est Département	Porto-Novo
3. Sud-Quest Département	Lokossa
4. Centre Département	Abomey
5. Nord-Est Département	Parakou
6. Nord-Ouest Département	Natitingou
7. Porto-Novo Prefecture	Porto-Novo
8. Adjohon Prefecture	Adjohon
9. Sakegé Prefecture	Sakegé
10. Pobé Prefecture	Pobé
11. Kétou Prefecture	Kétou
12. Abomey Prefecture	Abomey
13. Calavi Prefecture	Calavi
14. Ouidah Prefecture	Ouidah

15.	Allada Prefecture	Allada
16.	Athiémé Prefecture	Athiémé
17.	Atlahoué Prefecture	Atlahoué
18.	Grand-Popo Prefecture	Grand-Popo
19.	Bota Prefecture	Bota
20.	Savé Prefecture	Savé
21.	Zagnanado Prefecture	Zagnanado
22.	Savalou Prefecture	Savalou
23.	Dassa-Zouma Prefecture	Dassa-Zouma
24.	Parakou Prefecture	Parakou
25.	Bembéréké Prefecture	Bembéréké
26.	Kandi Prefecture	Kandi
27.	Séggana Prefecture	Séggana
28.	Banekoura Prefecture	Banekoura
29.	Malanville Prefecture	Malanville
30.	Nikki Prefecture	Nikki
31.	Natitingou Prefecture	Natitingou
32.	Boukombé Prefecture	Boukombé
33.	Tanguiéta Prefecture	Tanguiéta
34.	Kouandé Prefecture	Kouandé
35.	Djougou Prefecture	Djougou

Denmark (popular name)

The Kingdom of Denmark (official name)

"Kongeriget Danmark" (native name)

Copenhagen (national capital)

Denmark is located in Northwestern Europe. It is bounded
by the North Sea on the west; by Norway on the north;
by Sweden on the east; and by West Germany on the south.

The Major Administrative Divisions of Denmark number 24:
the 22 counties or "amter" and the 2 external dependencies.

The minor administrative divisions of Denmark comprise 6
county council districts or "amstradskredse;" 88 municipalities or "købstraeder;" 1300 rural municipalities or
"sognekommuner;" and over 2000 parishes or "kirkesogne."

Major Administrative Div.	Capitals of Major Adm. Div.
1. Åbenrå-Sønderborg Amt	Åbenrå
2. Ålborg Amt	Ålborg
3. Århus Amt	Århus

41

Denmark (continued)

Major Administrative Div.	Capitals of Major Adm. Div.
4. Bornholm Amt	Rønne
5. Københavns Amt	Københavns
6. Fredericksborg Amt	Hillerød
7. Haderslev Amt	Haderslev
8. Hjørring Amt	Hjørring
9. Holbaek Amt	Holbaek
10. Maribo Amt	Maribo
11. Odense Amt	Odense
12. Praestø Amt	Praestø
13. Randers Amt	Randers
14. Ribe Amt	Ribe
15. Ringkøbing Amt	Ringkøbing
16. Skandersborg Amt	Skandersborg
17. Sorø Amt	Sorø
18. Svendborg Amt	Svendborg
19. Thisted Amt	Thisted
20. Vejle Amt	Vejle
21. Viborg Amt	Viborg
22. Tønder Amt	Tønder
23. Grønland (Greenland)	Godthaab
24. Faerøerne (Faroe Islands)	Thórshavn

Further notes on the dependencies of Denmark:

Greenland is divided administratively into 3 provinces or "lansdele" and 19 townships or "byer."

The Faroe Islands have 7 regions or "syssel."

Dominican Republic
(popular and official name)

"Republica Dominica" (native name)

Santo Domingo (national capital)

The Dominican Republic is located in Southeastern North America, on the Island of Hispaniola of the Greater Antilles. It is bounded by Haiti on the west; by the Atlantic Ocean on the north and east; and by the Caribbean Sea on the south.

The Major Administrative Divisions of the Dominican Republic number 26: the 25 Provinces and the one National District.

Major Administrative Div.	Capitals of Major Adm. Div.
1. Pedernales Province	Pedernales
2. Barahona Province	Santa Cruz de Barahona
3. Independencia Province	Jimaní
4. San Rafael Province	Elias Piña
5. Baoruco Province	Neiba
6. Benefactor Province	San Juan
7. Azua Province	Azua de Compostella
8. Libertador Province	Dajabón
9. Monte Cristi Province	Monte Cristi
10. Puerto Plata Province	Puerto Plata
11. Valverde Province	Valverde
12. Santiago Province	Santiago de los Caballeros
13. Espaillat Province	Moca
14. Trinidad Sanchez Nogua Province	Trinidad Sanchez Nogua
15. Samaná Province	Samaná
16. El Seibo Province	El Seibo
17. La Romana Province	La Romana
18. San Pedro de Macorís Province	San Pedro de Macorís
19. San Cristobál Province	San Cristobál
20. Peravia Province	Baní
21. La Vega Province	La Vega
22. Sanchez Ramirez Prov.	Cotui
23. Duarte Province	San Francisco de Macoris
24. Salcedo Province	Salcedo
25. Santiago Rodriguez Prov.	Santiago Rodriguez
26. "Distrito Nacional"	Santo Domingo

Ecuador (popular name)

The Republic of Ecuador (official name)

"La Republica del Ecuador" (native name)

Quito (national capital)

Ecuador is located in Northwestern South America. It is
bounded by Colombia on the north; by Peru on the east
and south; and by the Pacific Ocean on the west.

The Major Administrative Divisions of Colombia number 20:
the 19 Provinces and the one National Territory.

The minor administrative divisions of Colombia are the 46
cantons and the 787 parishes.

Ecuador (continued)

Major Administrative Div.	Capitals of Major Adm. Div.
1. Azuay Province	Cuenca
2. Bolívar Province	Guaranda
3. Cañar Province	Azogues
4. Carchi Province	Tulcán
5. Chimborazo Province	Riobamba
6. Cotopaxi Province	Latacunga
7. El Oro Province	Machala
8. Esmeraldas Province	Esmeraldes
9. Guayas Province	Guayaquil
10. Imbabura Province	Ibarra
11. Loja Province	Loja
12. Los Ríos Province	Babahoyo
13. Manabi Province	Portoviejo
14. Napo Province	Tena
15. Pichincha Province	Quito
16. Santiago Morona Province	Mocas
17. Tungurahua Province	Ambato
18. Zamora-Chinchipe Province	Zamora
19. Pastaza Province	Puyo
20. The Colon National Territory (Galápagos)	San Cristóbal

El Salvador (popular name)

The Republic of El Salvador (official name)

"La Republica de El Salvador" (native name)

San Salvador (national capital)

El Salvador is located in Southern North America, in the
area known as Central America. It is bounded by Guatemala on the west; by Honduras and the Gulf of Fonseca
on the north and east; and by the Pacific Ocean on the
south.

The Major Administrative Divisions of El Salvador are the
14 Departments.

The minor administrative divisions of El Salvador are the
260 districts or "municipios."

Departments	Capitals of Departments
1. Ahuachapán	Ahuachapán

44

2.	Cabañas	Sensuntepeque
3.	Chalatenango	Chalatenango
4.	Cuscatlán	Cojutepeque
5.	La Libertad	Nueva San Salvador
6.	La Paz	Zacatecoluca
7.	La Unión	La Unión
8.	Morazán	San Francisco Gotera
9.	San Miguel	San Miguel
10.	San Salvador	San Salvador
11.	San Vicente	San Vicente
12.	Santa Ana	Santa Ana
13.	Sansonate	Sansonate
14.	Usulatán	Usulatán

Ethiopia (popular name)

The Ethiopian Empire (official name)

"Ya Ityopia Nigusa Nagast Mangist" (native name)

Addis Ababa (nationalist capital)

Ethiopia is located in Northeastern Africa. It is bounded by the Red Sea on the northeast; by Somalia on the east; by Kenya on the south; and by Sudan on the west.

The Major Administrative Divisions of Ethiopia are the 14 Provinces or "taqlai-gizat."

The minor administrative divisions of Ethiopia are the 82 sub-provinces or "awrajji-gizat" and the many districts and sub-districts.

Major Administrative Div.	Capitals of Major Adm. Div.
1. Tigre Province	Makale
2. Begemder Province	Gondar
3. Gojjam Province	Debra Markos
4. Shoa Province	Addis Ababa
5. Wollo Province	Dessie
6. Hararge Province	Dire Dawa
7. Arussi Province	Aselle
8. Gemu Gofa Province	Chencha
9. Sidamo Province	Yirgalem
10. Kaffa Province	Jimma
11. Ilubabor Province	Gore
12. Wollega Province	Lekempti
13. Bale Province	Goba
14. Eritrea Province	Asmara

Finland (popular name)

The Republic of Finland (official name)

"Suomen Tasavalta" (native name)

Helsinki (national capital)

Finland is located in Northern Europe. It is bounded by Norway on the north; by the U. S. S. R. on the east; by the Gulf of Finland, the U. S. S. R. , and the Baltic Sea on the south; and by the Gulf of Bothnia, Sweden, and Norway on the west.

The Major Administrative Divisions of Finland are the 12 Provinces or "lääni. "

The minor administrative divisions of Finland are the 252 sheriff's districts and the urban and rural councils.

Provinces	Provincial Capitals
1. Ahvenanmaan	Maarianhamina
2. Lapin	Rovaniemi
3. Oulun	Oulun
4. Vaasan	Vaasan
5. Kuopion	Kuopion
6. Mikhelin	Mikhelin
7. Hämeen	Tampere
8. Turunja-Porin	Turku
9. Keski-Suomen	Jyväskyla
10. Pohjois-Karjalan	Joensuu
11. Kymen	Kouvola
12. Uodenmaan	Helsinki

France (popular name)

The French Republic (official name)

"La République Française" (native name)

Paris (national capital)

France is located in Northwestern Europe. It is bounded by Belgium, Luxembourg, and West Germany on the east and northeast; by Switzerland and Italy on the east; by Monaco, the Mediterranean Sea, Spain, and Andorra on the south; and by the Bay of Biscay, the Atlantic Ocean, and the English Channel on the west.

The Major Administrative Divisions of France number 102:
the 90 metropolitan "départements"
the 4 overseas departments or "départements outremers"
and the 8 overseas territories or "territoires outremers"

The minor administrative divisions include the 313 metropolitan "arrondissements," as well as numerous cantons and communes.

Major Administrative Div.	Capitals of Major Adm. Div.
1. Ain Département	Bourg
2. Aisne Département	Laon
3. Allier Département	Moulins
4. Basses-Alpes Département	Digne
5. Hautes-Alpes Département	Gap
6. Alpes-Maritimes Département	Nice
7. Ardèche Département	Privas
8. Ardennes Département	Mézières
9. Ariège Département	Foix
10. Aube Département	Troyes
11. Aude Département	Carcassonne
12. Aveyron Département	Rodez
13. Bouches-du-Rhône Département	Marseille
14. Calvados Département	Caen
15. Cantal Département	Aurillac
16. Charente Département	Angoulême
17. Charente-Maritime Département	Bourges
18. Cher Département	Tulle
19. Corrèze Département	Tulle
20. Corse Département	Ajaccio
21. Côte-du-Nord Département	Saint-Briene
22. Creuse Département	Guéret
23. Dordogne Département	Périgueux
24. Doubs Département	Besançon
25. Drôme Département	Valence
26. Eure Département	Evseux
27. Eure-et-Loir Département	Chartres
28. Finistere Département	Quimper
29. Gard Département	Nîmes
30. Haut-Garanne Département	Toulouse
31. Gers Département	Auch
32. Gironde Département	Bordeaux
33. Herault Département	Montpellier
34. Ílle-et-Vilaine Département	Rennes
35. Indre Département	Châteauroux
36. Indre-et-Loire Département	Tours
37. Isere Département	Grenoble

France (continued)

Major Administrative Div.	Capitals of Major Adm. Div.
38. Jura Département	Lons-le-Saunier
39. Landes Département	Mont-de-Marsan
40. Loir-et-Cher Département	Blois
41. Loire Département	Saint-Etienne
42. Loire-Atlantique Département	Nantes
43. Haute-Loire Département	Le Puy
44. Loiret Département	Orléans
45. Lot Département	Cahors
46. Lot-et-Garonne Département	Agen
47. Lozere Département	Mende
48. Maine-et-Loire Département	Angers
49. Manche Département	Coutances
50. Marne Département	Châlons-sur-Marne
51. Haute-Marne Département	Chaumont
52. Mayenne Département	Laval
53. Meurthe-et-Moselle Département	Nancy
54. Meuse Département	Bar-le-Duc
55. Morbihan Département	Vannes
56. Moselle Département	Metz
57. Nievre Département	Nevers
58. Nord Département	Lille
59. Oise Département	Beauvais
60. Orne Département	Alençon
61. Pas-de-Calais Département	Arras
62. Puy-de-Dôme Département	Clermont-Ferrand
63. Basses-Pyrénées Département	Pau
64. Hautes-Pyrénées	Tarbes
65. Pyrénées Orientales Département	Perpignan
66. Bas-Rhin Département	Strasbourg
67. Haut-Rhin Département	Colmar
68. Rhône Département	Lyon
69. Haute-Saône Département	Vesoul
70. Saône-et-Loire Département	Mâcon
71. Sarthe Département	Le Mans
72. Savoie Département	Chambérg
73. Haute-Savoie Département	Annecy
74. Seine Département	Paris
75. Seine-Maritime Département	Rouen
76. Seine-et-Marne Département	Melun
77. Seine-et-Oise Département	Versailles
78. Deux-Sevres Département	Niort
79. Somme Département	Amiens
80. Tarn Département	Albi
81. Tarn-et-Garonne Département	Montauban
82. Var Département	Draguignan

83.	Vaucluse Département	Avignon
84.	Vendée Département	La Roche-sur-Yon
85.	Vienne Département	Poitiers
86.	Haute-Vienne Département	Limoges
87.	Vosges Département	Epinal
88.	Yonne Département	Auxerre
89.	Territoire-de-Belfort	Belfort
90.	Côte-d'Or Département	Dijon
91.	Martinique Département Outremer	Fort-de-France
92.	Guadeloupe Département Outremer	Basse-Terre
93.	Île de la Réunion Département Outremer	Saint-Denis
94.	La Guyane Française (French Guiana) Département Outremer	Cayenne
95.	Polynésie Française Territoire Outremer (French Polynesia)	Papeete
96.	Nouvelle Caledonie Territoire Outremer (New Caledonia)	Nouméa
97.	Territoire Outremer des Comores (Comoro Archipelago)	Maroni
98.	Côte Française des Somalie Territoire Outremer (French Somaliland)	Djibouti
99.	Îles St.-Pierre et Miquelon Territoire Outremer	St.-Pierre
100.	Îles Wallis et Futuna Territoire Outremer	Mata-Utu
101.	Terres Australes et Antarctiques Françaises (French Southern and Antarctic Lands)	Port-aux-Français
102.	Nouvelles Hébrides Territoire Outremer (New Hebrides Condominium)	Port-Vila

Further notes on minor administrative divisions of the external possessions:

Polynésie Française is divided into 5 circomscriptions:
(adm. seats)

1.	Iles du Vent	Papeete
2.	Îles sous le Vent	Utorua, Raiatéa Island
3.	Tuámotu Group	Rangiroa
4.	Austral Islands	Rurutu Island
5.	Marquesas Islands	Tai-o-Hae, Nuku-Hiva Island

Côte Française des Somalis is divided into 4 districts:
1. Djibouti

France (continued)

    2. Tadjoura
    3. Ali Sabieh
    4. Dikhil

Territoire des Comores is divided into 4 districts:

1. Île Mayotte	Dzaoudzi
2. Île Anjouan	Mutsamudu
3. Île Grand Comore	Maroni
4. Île Mohéli	Fomboni

Martinique is divided into 2 arrondessements which are sub-divided into 34 communes.

Guadeloupe is divided into Basse Terre and Point-à-Petre Arrondessements which are subdivided into cantons and communes.

Île de la Réunion has 23 communes.

La Guyane Française consists of 14 communes plus Cayenne and Inini (arrondessements)

Îles St. Pierre and Miquelon have 2 communes
    1. St.-Pierre
    2. Miquelon-Langlade

Gabon (popular name)

The Republic of Gabon (official name)

"République Gabonaise" (native name)

Libreville (national capital)

Gabon is located in Western Africa. It is bounded by Cameroon on the north; by Congo (Brazzaville) on the east and south; and by the Atlantic Ocean on the west.

The Major Administrative Divisions of Gabon number 37: the 9 Prefectures and the 28 Sub-Prefectures.

The minor administrative divisions are the communes and the administrative stations.

Major Administrative Div.	Capitals of Major Adm. Div.
1. Ogooué-Maritîme Prefecture	Port-Gentil
2. Estuaire Prefecture	Libreville
3. Woleu-N'Tem Prefecture	Oyem
4. Ogooué-Ivindo Prefecture	Makokou
5. Moyen-Ogooué Prefecture	Lambaréné
6. Ogooué-Lolo Prefecture	Koula-Moutou
7. Haut-Ogooué Prefecture	Franceville
8. N'Gounié Prefecture	Mouila
9. Nyanga Prefecture	Tchibanga
10. Port-Gentil Sub-Prefecture	Port-Gentil
11. Libreville Sub-Prefecture	Libreville
12. Coco Beach Sub-Prefecture	Coco Beach
13. Kiango Sub-Prefecture	Kiango
14. Omboué Sub-Prefecture	Omboué
15. Lambaréné Sub-Prefecture	Lambaréné
16. N'djole Sub-Prefecture	N'djole
17. Mouila Sub-Prefecture	Mouila
18. M'Bigou Sub-Prefecture	M'Bigou
19. Mimongo Sub-Prefecture	Mimongo
20. Fougamou Sub-Prefecture	Fougamou
21. N'Dendé Sub-Prefecture	N'Dendé
22. Tchibanga Sub-Prefecture	Tchibanga
23. Mayunba Sub-Prefecture	Mayumba
24. Moabi Sub-Prefecture	Moabi
25. Makokou Sub-Prefecture	Makokou
26. Booué Sub-Prefecture	Booué
27. Mekambo Sub-Prefecture	Mekambo
28. Koula-Moutou Sub-Prefecture	Koula-Moutou
29. Lastoursville Sub-Prefecture	Lastoursville
30. Franceville Sub-Prefecture	Franceville
31. Okondja Sub-Prefecture	Okondja
32. Moanda Sub-Prefecture	Moanda
33. Oyem Sub-Prefecture	Oyem
34. Bitam Sub-Prefecture	Bitam
35. Medouneu Sub-Prefecture	Medouneu
36. Minvoul Sub-Prefecture	Minvoul
37. Mitzic Sub-Prefecture	Mitzic

Gambia (popular name)

The Government of the Gambia (official name)

Bathurst (national capital)

Gambia is located in Western Africa. It is bounded by the Atlantic Ocean on the west; and by Senegal on the north, east and south.

Gambia (continued)

The Major Administrative Divisions of Gambia number 6:
the 4 Commissioner's Divisions and the 2 Municipalities.

The minor administrative divisions are the 35 districts and
6 area councils.

Major Administrative Div.	Capitals of Major Adm. Div.
1. Western Division	Brikama
2. Central Division	Mansa Konko
3. MacCarthy Division	Georgetown
4. Upper River Division	Basse
5. Kombo Municipality	Kombo
6. Bathurst Municipality	Bathurst

(Germany) East Germany (popular name)

The German Democratic Republic (official name)

"Deutsche Demokratische Republik" (native name)

East Berlin (national capital)

East Germany is located in Eastern Europe. It is bounded
by the Baltic Sea on the north; by Poland on the east;
by Czechoslovakia and West Germany on the south; and
by West Germany on the west.

The Major Administrative Divisions of East Germany are the
14 Administrative Districts or "bezirken."

The minor administrative divisions of East Germany are the
216 counties or "kreise" and the 9190 communities.

Administrative Districts	Capitals of the Adm. Districts
1. Potsdam	Potsdam
2. Schwerin	Schwerin
3. Neubrandenburg	Neubrandenburg
4. Karlmarxstadt	Karlmarxstadt
5. Dresden	Dresden
6. Leipzig	Leipzig
7. Halle	Halle
8. Magdeburg	Magdeburg
9. Cottbus	Cottbus
10. Frankfurt	Frankfurt
11. Erfurt	Erfurt
12. Gera	Gera

| 13. Guhl | Guhl |
| 14. Rostock | Rostock |

(Germany) West Germany (popular name)

The Federal Republic of Germany (official name)

"Bundesrepublik Deutschland" (native name)

Bonn (national capital)

West Germany is located in Central Europe. It is bounded by the North Sea and Denmark on the north; by East Germany and Czechoslovakia on the east; by Switzerland and Austria on the south; and by France, Luxembourg, Belgium, the Netherlands and the North Sea on the west.

The Major Administrative Divisions of West Germany are the 11 States or "laender."

The minor administrative divisions of West Germany are the administrative areas or "regierungsbezirken," the urban districts or "stadtkreis," the rural districts or "landkries," and the communes or "gemeinde."

	States	State Capitals
1.	West Berlin	West Berlin
2.	Bayern	Munich
3.	Baden-Württemburg	Stuttgart
4.	Hessen	Weisbaden
5.	Rheinland-Pfalz	Mainz
6.	Nordrhein-Westfalen	Düsseldorf
7.	Niedersachsen	Hanover
8.	Schleswig-Holstein	Kiel
9.	Saarland	Saarbrücken
10.	Hamburg	Hamburg
11.	Bremen	Bremen

Further notes on minor administrative divisions:

Baden-Württemburg has 4 areas and 72 districts.

Bayern has 7 areas and 191 districts.

Hamburg has 7 districts.

West Germany (continued)

Hessen has 3 areas and 48 districts.

Niedersachsen has 8 districts and 60 urban districts.

Nordrhein-Westfalen has 6 areas and 95 districts.

Schleswig-Holstein has 21 districts.

Ghana (popular name)

The Republic of Ghana (official name)

Accra (national capital)

Ghana is located in Western Africa. It is bounded by Upper
Volta on the north; by Togo on the east; by the Atlantic
Ocean on the south; and by the Ivory Coast on the west.

The Major Administrative Divisions of Ghana are the 8 Administrative Regions.

The minor administrative divisions of Ghana are the districts
and the municipal councils.

Administrative Regions	Capitals of Adm. Regions
1. Western	Sekondi
2. Eastern	Koforidua
3. Upper	Bolgatanga
4. Northern	Tamale
5. Volta	Ho
6. Ashanti	Kumasi
7. Brong-Ahofo	Sunyani
8. Central	Cape Coast

Greece (popular name)

The Kingdom of Greece (official name)

"Vasileion Tis Ellados" (native name)

Athens (national capital)

Greece is located in Southern Europe. It is bounded by Albania on the northwest; by Yugoslavia and Bulgaria on the
north; by Turkey on the northeast; by the Aegian Sea on
the east; by the Mediterranean Sea on the south; and by

the Ionian Sea on the west.

The Major Administrative Divisions of Greece are the 52 Departments or "nomoi."

The minor administrative divisions are the 147 districts or "eparchies."

Departments	Capitals of Departments
1. Aitoliakai Akarnania	Mesolongion
2. Akhaia	Patras
3. Argolis	Nauplia
4. Arta	Arta
5. Attiki	Athens
6. Ayion Oros (Mt. Athos)	Karyai
7. Boeotia	Levadeia
8. Dhodhikanisos	Rhodes
9. Drama	Drama
10. Evritania	Karpenissi
11. Evros	Alexandroupolis
12. Euboea	Chalcis
13. Florina	Florina
14. Fokis	Amphissa
15. Fthiotis	Lamia
16. Ilia	Pyrgos
17. Imanthia	Verria
18. Ioannina	Ionnina
19. Iraklion	Candia
20. Kardhitsa	Kardhitsa
21. Kastoria	Kastoria
22. Kavalla	Kavalla
23. Kefallinia	Argostolion
24. Kerkira	Kerkira
25. Arkadhia	Tripolis
26. Khalkidhiki	Polyghyros
27. Khania	Khania
28. Khios	Khios
29. Kikladhes	Hermoupolis
30. Kilkis	Kilkis
31. Korinthos	Korinthos
32. Kozani	Kozani
33. Lakonia	Sparta
34. Larissa	Larissa
35. Lasithi	Hagios Nikolaos
36. Lesvos	Mytilene
37. Levkas	Levkas
38. Magnisia	Volos

Greece (continued)

Departments	Capitals of Departments
39. Messinia	Kalamata
40. Pella	Edessa
41. Pieria	Katerini
42. Preveza	Preveza
43. Rethymnon	Rethymnon
44. Rodhopi	Komotini
45. Samos	Limon Vatheos
46. Serrai	Serrai
47. Thesprotia	Hegoumenitsa
48. Thessaloniki	Salonika
49. Trikkala	Trikkala
50. Xanthi	Xanthi
51. Zakinthos	Zante
52. Corfu	Corfu

Guatemala (popular name)

The Republic of Guatemala (official name)

"La República de Guatemala (native name)

Guatemala City (national capital)

Guatemala is located in Southern North America, in the area known as Central or Middle America. It is bounded by Mexico on the west and north; by British Honduras and El Salvador on the east and south; and by the Pacific Ocean on the southwest.

The Major Administrative Divisions of Guatemala are the 22 Departments or "departamentos."

The minor administrative divisions are the 322 municipalities or "municipios."

Departments	Capitals of Departments
1. Alta Verapaz	Cobán
2. Baja Verapaz	Salamá
3. Chimaltenango	Chimaltenango
4. Chiquumula	Chiquumula
5. El Petén	Flores
6. El Progreso	El Progreso
7. El Quiché	Santa Cruz del Quiché
8. Escuintla	Escuintla

9.	Guatemala	Guatemala City
10.	Huehuetenango	Huehuetenango
11.	Izabel	Puerto Barrios
12.	Jalapa	Jalapa
13.	Jutiapa	Jutiapa
14.	Quezaltenango	Quezaltenengo
15.	Retalhuleu	Retalhuleu
16.	Sacatepequez	Antigua Guatemala
17.	San Marcos	San Marcos
18.	Santa Rosa	Cuilapa
19.	Sololá	Solalá
20.	Suchitepéquez	Mazatenango
21.	Totonicapán	Totonicapán
22.	Zacapa	Zacapa

Guinea (popular name)

The Republic of Guinea (official name)

"République de Guinée" (native name)

Conakry (national capital)

Guinea is located in West Africa. It is bounded by Senegal and Mali on the north; by the Ivory Coast on the east; by Liberia on the south; and by the Atlantic Ocean on the west.

The Major Administrative Divisions of Guinea are the 29 "Régions."

The minor administrative divisions of Guinea are the "arrondissements" and the "communes."

	Regions	Capitals of Régions
1.	N'zérékore	N'zérékore
2.	Macenta	Macenta
3.	Beyla	Beyla
4.	Guékédou	Guékédou
5.	Kissidougou	Kissidougou
6.	Kankan	Kankan
7.	Siguiri	Siguiri
8.	Kouroussa	Kouroussa
9.	Faranah	Faranah
10.	Dalaba	Dalaba
11.	Tougué	Tougué
12.	Labé	Labé

Guinea (continued)

Régions	Capitals of Régions
13. Dabola	Dabola
14. Dinguiraye	Dinguiraye
15. Mamou	Mamou
16. Pita	Pita
17. Mali	Mali
18. Kindia	Kindia
19. Télimélé	Télimélé
20. Gaoual	Gaoual
21. Youkoukoun	Youkoukoun
22. Forécariah	Forécariah
23. Conakry	Conakry
24. Dubréka	Dubréka
25. Boffa	Boffa
26. Boké	Boké
27. Fria	Fria
28. Kerouane	Kerouane
29. Yomou	Yomou

Haiti (popular name)

The Republic of Haiti (official name)

"La République d'Haiti" (native name)

Port-au-Prince (national capital)

Haiti is located in Southeastern North America, on the island of Hispaniola in the Greater Antilles. It is bounded by the Dominican Republic on the east, and by the Atlantic Ocean on the south, west, and north.

The Major Administrative Divisions of Haiti are the 9 Departments or "départements."

The minor administrative divisions of Haiti are the 26 "arrondissements," over 300 "communes," and the numerous "rural sections."

Départments	Capitals of Départments
1. Nord	Cap-Haitien
2. Nord-Est	Fort Liberté
3. Nord-Ouest	Port-de-Paix
4. Artibonite	Gonaives
5. Centrale	Hinche
6. Ouest	Port-au-Prince

58

7. Sud-Est	Jacmel
8. Sud	Les Cayes
9. Grand Anse	Jeremie

Honduras (popular name)

The Republic of Honduras (official name)

"Republica de Honduras" (native name)

Tegucigalpa (national capital)

Honduras is located in Southern North America, in the area known as Central or Middle America. It is bounded by the Caribbean Sea on the north; by Nicaragua on the east and south; by El Salvador on the south and southwest; and by Guatemala on the west.

The Major Administrative Divisions of Honduras number 19: the 17 Departments; the one Territory, and the one "Distrito Central."

The minor administrative divisions of Honduras are the districts and the 278 municipalities.

Major Administrative Div.	Capitals of Major Adm. Div.
1. Atlantida Department	La Ceiba
2. Choluteca Department	Choluteca
3. Colón Department	Trujillo
4. Comayagua Department	Comayagua
5. Copán Department	Santa Rosa de Copán
6. Cortés Department	San Pedro Sula
7. El Paráiso Department	Yuscarán
8. Francisco Morzán Department	Tegucigalpa
9. Intibucá Department	La Esperanza
10. Isla de la Bahía Department	Roatán
11. La Paz Department	La Paz
12. Lempira Department	Graciás
13. Ocotepeque Department	Nueva Ocotepeque
14. Olancho Department	Juticalpa
15. Santa Bárbara Department	Santa Bárbara
16. Valle Department	Nacoame
17. Yoro Department	Yoro
18. The Mosquito Coast Territory	Tegucigalpa
19. "Distrito Central"	Tegucigalpa

Hungary (popular name)

The Hungarian People's Republic (official name)

"Magyar Népköztársaság" (native name)

Budapest (national capital)

Hungary is located in Central Europe. It is bounded by
Czechoslovakia and the U. S. S. R. on the north; by Yugoslavia on the south; by Rumania on the east; and by Austria on the west.

The Major Administrative Divisions of Hungary number 24:
the 19 Counties or "megyék;" and the 5 County Boroughs.

The minor administrative divisions are the 128 districts and
the 1310 communes.

Major Administrative Div.	Capitals of Major Adm. Div.
1. Bács-Kiskum County	Kecskemét
2. Baranya County	Pécs
3. Békés County	Békéscsaba
4. Borsod-Abúj-Zamplén County	Miskolc
5. Csongrád County	Hodmezővasárhely
6. Györ-Sopron County	Györ
7. Hajdu-Bihar County	Debrecen
8. Heves County	Eger
9. Komárom County	Tatabanya
10. Nógrád County	Salgotarjan
11. Pest County	Budapest
12. Somogy County	Kaposvar
13. Szabolcs-Szatmár County	Nyiregyhaza
14. Szolnok County	Szolnok
15. Tolna County	Tolna
16. Fejer County	Székesfehervár
17. Veszprém County	Veszprém
18. Zala County	Zalaegerszeg
19. Vas County	Szombathely
20. Budapest County Borough	Budapest
21. Miskolc County Borough	Miskolc
22. Debrecen County Borough	Debrecen
23. Pécs County Borough	Pécs
24. Szeged County Borough	Szeged

Iceland (popular name)

The Republic of Iceland (official name)

"Lýdveldid Ísland" (native name)

Reykjavik (national capital)

Iceland is located off the northwest part of Europe and is grouped usually with the countries of the European Continent. It is an island republic just south of the Arctic Circle in the North Atlantic Ocean.

The Major Administrative Divisions of Iceland number 38: the 23 Districts or "sýslur;" the 14 Independent Towns or "kaupstaoir;" and the Capital City of Reykjavik.

The minor administrative divisions of Iceland are the 214 communes or "hreppur."

Major Administrative Div.	Capitals of Major Adm. Div.
1. Gullbringu District	Gullbringu
2. Kjósar District	Kjósar
3. Borgarfjarðar District	Borgarnes
4. Mýrar District	Borgarnes
5. Snaefellsnes District	Stykkisholmur
6. Dala District	Búdardalur
7. Au-Baroastrandar District	Patreksfjordur
8. V.-Baroastrandar District	Patreksfjórdur
9. V.-Isafjaroar District	Isafjaroar
10. N.-Isafjaroar District	Isafjaroar
11. Stranda District	Hólmavík
12. V.-Húnavatns District	Blönduós
13. Au-Húnavatns District	Blönduós
14. Skagafjaroar District	Skagafjaroar
15. Eyjafjaroar District	Eyjafjaroar
16. S.-Pingeyjar District	Pingeyjar
17. N.-Pingeyjar District	Pingeyjar
18. N.-Múla District	Múla
19. S.-Múla District	Eskifjördur
20. Au-Skaftafells District	Vik i Mýrdal
21. V.-Skaftafells District	Vik i Mýrdal
22. Rangárvalla District	Hvolsvöllur
23. Arnes District	Selfoss
24. Reykjavik Independent Town	Reykjavik
25. Kópavogur Independent Town	Kópavogur
26. Hafnarfjórur Independent Town	Hafnarfjórur

Iceland (continued)

Major Administrative Div.	Capitals of Major Adm. Div.
27. Keflavik Independent Town	Keflavik
28. Akranes Independent Town	Akranes
29. Ísafjórour Independent Town	Ísafjórour
30. Sauoárkrókur Independent Town	Sauoárkrókur
31. Siglufjórour Independent Town	Siglufjórour
32. Olafsjórour Independent Town	Olafsjórour
33. Akureyri Independent Town	Akureyri
34. Húsavik Independent Town	Húsavik
35. Seyoisfjórour Independent Town	Seyoisfjórour
36. Neskaupstaour Independent Town	Neskaupstaour
37. Vestmannaeyjar Independent Town	Vestmannaeyjar
38. Capital of Reykjavik	Reykjavik

India (popular name)

The Sovereign Democratic Republic of India (official name)

"Lokatantratnak Gamarajya Bharat" (native name)

New Delhi (national capital)

India is located in Eastern Asia. It is bounded by Burma
and the Bay of Bengal on the east; by the Indian Ocean
and Ceylon on the south; by the Arabian Sea on the west;
by Pakistan on the northwest; and by China, Nepal, Sikkim, and Bhutan on the north.

The Major Administrative Divisions of India number 26:
the 16 States, the 9 Federal Territories; and the one
Frontier Tract.

The minor administrative divisions are the 326 districts, the
numerous municipalities, city corporations, and village
and block "panchayets."

Major Administrative Div.	Capitals of Major Adm. Div.
1. Andhra Pradesh State	Hyderabad
2. Assam State	Shillong
3. Bihar State	Patna
4. Jammu and Kashmir State	Srinagar
5. Kerala State	Trivandrum
6. Madhya Pradesh State	Bhopal
7. Madras State	Madras
8. Mysore State	Bangalore

9.	Orissa State	Bhubaneswar
10.	Punjab State	Chandigarh
11.	Rajasthan State	Jaipur
12.	Uttar Pradesh State	Lucknow
13.	West Bengal State	Calcutta
14.	Gujarat State	Ahmedabad
15.	Maharashtra State	Bombay
16.	Nagaland State	Kohima
17.	Goa, Daman, and Diu Territory	Panjim
18.	Dadra and Nagar Haveli Terr.	Silvassa
19.	Andaman and Nicobar Islands Territory	Port Blair
20.	Delhi Territory	Delhi
21.	Himachel Pradesh Territory	Simla
22.	Manipur Territory	Imphal
23.	Tripura Territory	Agartala
24.	Lacadive, Amindive and Minicoy Island Territory	Kavaratti
25.	Pondicherry Territory	Pondicherry
26.	North-East Frontier Tract	Shillong

Indonesia (popular name)

The Republic of Indonesia (official name)

"Republik Indonesia" (native name)

Jakarta (national capital)

Indonesia is located in Southeast Asia.   It is the world's
largest archipelago.   It was formerly called the Dutch
East Indies, lying in the southwest Pacific, and facing
Malaysia and the Philippines on the north and Australia
on the south.

The Major Administrative Divisions of Indonesia number 22:
the 20 Provinces or "propinsi" and the 2 Special Cities.

The minor administrative divisions of Indonesia are the districts or "kabupaten."

Major Administrative Div.	Capitals of Major Adm. Div.
1. Atjeh Province	Kotoradja
2. North Sumatra Province	Medan
3. West Sumatra Province	Bukittinggi
4. Riauw Province	Pakan Baru
5. Djambi Province	Djambi

Indonesia (continued)

Major Administrative Div.	Capitals of Major Adm. Div.
6. South Sumatra Province	Palembang
7. West Java Province	Bandung
8. Central Java Province	Semarang
9. East Java Province	Surabaya
10. West Kalimantan Province	Pontianak
11. South Kalimantan Province	Bandjarmasin
12. East Kalimantan	Sarmarinda
13. Central Kalimantan Province	Palangka Raja
14. North Sulawesi Province	Menado
15. South Sulawesi Province	Makassar
16. West Nusa-Tenggara Province	Mataram
17. East Nusa-Tenggara Province	Kupang
18. Malaku Province	Ambon
19. Bali Province	Singaradja
20. Irian Barat Province	Kota Baru
21. The Special Autonomous District of Djokjakarta	Djokjakarta
22. The Metropolitan District of Jakarta-Rayn	Jakarta

Iran (popular name)

The Imperial Government of Iran (official name)

"Keshvar-e-Shahanshahi-Ye-Iran" (native name)

Teheran (national capital)

Iran is located in Southwestern Asia. It is bounded by the
U.S.S.R. and the Caspian Sea on the north; by Afghanistan and Pakistan on the east; by the Persian Gulf and the
Gulf of Oman on the south; and by Iraq and Turkey on
the west.

The Major Administrative Divisions of Iran number 13: the
12 Provinces or "ostán" and the one Capital City.

The minor administrative divisions of Iran are the 76 counties or "shahrestan."

Major Administrative Div.	Capitals of Major Adm. Div.
1. Gilan Province	Resht
2. Mazandaran Province	Sari
3. Eastern Azerbaijan Province	Tabriz
4. Western Azerbaijan Province	Rezaiyeh

5.	Kermanshah Province	Kermanshah
6.	Khuzistan Province	Ahwaz
7.	Fars Province	Shiraz
8.	Kerman Province	Kerman
9.	Khuristan Province	Meshed
10.	Isfahan Province	Isfahan
11.	Kurdistan Province	Sannandaj
12.	Baluchistan Province	Zahedan
13.	Capital City	Teheran

Iraq (popular name)

The Mesopotamiam Republic of Iraq (official name)

"Al Jamhouriyah Al Iraquia Mesopotamia" (native name)

Baghdad (national capital)

Iraq is located in southwestern Asia. It is bounded by Turkey on the north; by Iran on the east; by the Persian Gulf, Kuwait, and Saudi Arabia on the south; and by Jordan and Syria on the west.

The Major Administrative Divisions of Iraq number 15: the 14 Provinces or "liwa" and the 1 Neutral Zone.

The minor administrative divisions of Iraq are called "qadhas" and the subdivisions of "qadhas" are called "nahyahs."

	Provinces	Provincial Capitals
1.	Amara Province	Amara
2.	Arbil Province	Arbil
3.	Baghdad Province	Baghdad
4.	Basra Province	Basra
5.	Diyala Province	Diyala
6.	Diwaniya Province	Diwaniya
7.	Hilla Province	Hilla
8.	Karbela Province	Karbela
9.	Kirkuk Province	Kirkuk
10.	Kut Province	Kut
11.	Mosul Province	Mosul
12.	Nairiyah Province	Nairiyah
13.	Ramadi Province	Ramadi
14.	Sulaimaniya Province	Sulaimaniya
15.	The Iraqi-Saudi Arabian Neutral Zone	

Ireland (popular name)

The Republic of Ireland (official name)

"Poblach Na H'Eireann" (native name)

Dublin (national capital)

Ireland is located in northwestern Europe. It is bounded by
the Atlantic Ocean on the south, west, and northwest; by
the United Kingdom's Northern Ireland on the north and
northeast; and by the Irish Sea on the east.

The Major Administrative Divisions of Ireland number 31:
the 27 County Councils and the 4 County Borough Councils.

The minor administrative divisions of Ireland are the 56
urban county districts and the 28 town councils.

Major Administrative Div.	Capitals of Major Adm. Div.
1. Carlow County	Carlow
2. Cavan County	Cavan
3. Clare County	Clare
4. Cork County	Cork
5. Donegal County	Lifford
6. Dublin County	Dublin
7. Galway County	Galway
8. Kerry County	Tralee
9. Kildare County	Naas
10. Kilkenny County	Kilkenny
11. Lavis County	Portlaoise
12. Leitrim County	Carrick-On-Shannon
13. Limerick County	Limerick
14. Longford County	Longford
15. Louth County	Dundalk
16. Mayo County	Castlebar
17. Meath County	An Uaimh
18. Monaghan County	Monaghan
19. Offaly County	Tullamore
20. Roscommon County	Roscommon
21. Sligo County	Sligo
22. Waterford County	Dungarvan
23. Wicklow County	Wicklow
24. Tipperary County, No. Riding	Nenagh
25. Tipperary County, So. Riding	Clonmel
26. Westmeath County	Mullingar
27. Wexford County	Wexford

28. Cork County Borough
29. Dublin County Borough
30. Limerick County Borough
31. Waterford County Borough

Israel (popular name)

The State of Israel (official name)

"Medinat Israel" (native name)

Jerusalem (national capital)

Israel is located in southwestern Asia, in the area known as the Middle East or Asia Minor. It is bounded by the Mediterranean Sea on the west; by Lebanon and Syria on the north; by Jordan on the east; and by Egypt on the south.

The Major Administrative Divisions of Israel number 20: the 6 Administrative Districts and the 14 subdistricts.

The minor administrative divisions of Israel include 50 regional, 24 municipal, and 107 local councils.

Major Administrative Div.	Capitals of Major Adm. Div.
1. Jerusalem District	Jerusalem
2. Northern District	Tiberius
3. Haifa District	Haifa
4. Central District	Ramle
5. Tel-Aviv District	Tel-Aviv
6. Southern or Negev District	Beersheba
7. Jerusalem Subdistrict	Jerusalem
8. Safad Subdistrict	Safad
9. Kinneret Subdistrict	Kinneret
10. Jezreel Subdistrict	Jezreel
11. Acre Subdistrict	Acre
12. Haifa Subdistrict	Haifa
13. Hadera Subdistrict	Hadera
14. Sharon Subdistrict	Sharon
15. Petah-Tikva Subdistrict	Petah-Tikva
16. Ramle Subdistrict	Ramle
17. Tel-Aviv/Jaffa Subdistrict	Tel-Aviv
18. Ascalon Subdistrict	Ascalon
19. Rehvat Subdistrict	Rehvat
20. Beersheba Subdistrict	Beersheba

Italy (popular name)

The Italian Republic (official name)

"Republic Italiana" (native name)

Rome (national capital)

Italy is located in southern Europe, comprising a boot-shaped peninsula extended into the Mediterranean. It is bounded by Yugoslavia, the Adriatic Sea, and the Ionian Sea on the east; by the Tyrrhenian Sea on the south and southwest; by the Ligurian Sea and France on the west; and by Switzerland on the north.

The Major Administrative Divisions of Italy number 110. These are the 19 Regions or "compartimenti" and the 91 Provinces or "provincias."

The minor administrative divisions of Italy are the 8,029 communes.

Major Administrative Div.	Capitals of Major Adm. Div.
1. Abruzzo Molise Region	Aquila
2. Apulia Region	Bari
3. Basilicata Region	Potenza
4. Calabria Region	Reggio Calabria
5. Campania Region	Napoli (Naples)
6. Emilia-Romagna Region	Bologna
7. Friuli-Venezia-Giulia Region	Trieste
8. Lazio Region	Roma
9. Liguria Region	Genova (Genoa)
10. Lombardia Region	Milano (Milan)
11. Le Marche Region	Ancona
12. Piemonte Region	Torino (Turin)
13. Sardegna Region	Cagliari
14. Sicilia Region	Palermo
15. Toscana Region	Firenze (Florence)
16. Trentino-Alto Adige Region	Trento
17. Umbria Region	Perugia
18. Valle D'Aosta Region	Aosta
19. Veneto Region	Venezia (Venice)
20. Agrigento Province	Agrigento
21. Alessandria Province	Alessandria
22. Ancona Province	Ancona
23. Aosta Province	Aosta
24. Apuania Province	Apuania
25. Aquila Province	Aquila

26. Arezzo Province	Arezzo
27. Ascoli Piceno Province	Ascoli Piceno
28. Asti Province	Asti
29. Avelino Province	Avelino
30. Bari Province	Bari
31. Belluno Province	Belluno
32. Benevento Province	Benevento
33. Bergamo Province	Bergamo
34. Bologna Province	Bologna
35. Bolzano Province	Bolzano
36. Brescia Province	Brescia
37. Brindisi Province	Brindisi
38. Cagliari Province	Cagliari
39. Caltanissetta Province	Caltanissetta
40. Campobasso Province	Campobasso
41. Catania Province	Catania
42. Catanzaro Province	Catanzaro
43. Chieti Province	Chieti
44. Como Province	Como
45. Cosenza Province	Cosenza
46. Cremona Province	Cremona
47. Cuneo Province	Cuneo
48. Enna Province	Enna
49. Ferrara Province	Ferrano
50. Firenze Province	Firenze
51. Foggia Province	Foggia
52. Forli Province	Forli
53. Friuli Province	Friuli
54. Frosinone Province	Frosinone
55. Genova Province	Genova
56. Gorizia Province	Gorizia
57. Grosseto Province	Grosseto
58. Imperia Province	Imperia
59. Ionio Province	Taranto
60. La Spezia Province	La Spezia
61. Lecce Province	Lecce
62. Littoria Province	Littoria
63. Livorno Province	Livorno
64. Lucca Province	Lucca
65. Macerata Province	Macerata
66. Mantova Province	Mantova
67. Matera Province	Matera
68. Messina Province	Messina
69. Milano Province	Milano
70. Modena Province	Modena
71. Napoli Province	Napoli
72. Novara Province	Novara

Italy (continued)

Major Administrative Div.	Capitals of Major Adm. Div.
73. Nuoro Province	Nuoro
74. Padova Province	Padova
75. Palermo Province	Palermo
76. Parma Province	Parma
77. Pavia Province	Pavia
78. Perugia Province	Perugia
79. Pesaro e Urbino Province	Resaro
80. Pescara Province	Pescara
81. Piacenza Province	Piacenza
82. Pisa Province	Pisa
83. Pistoia Province	Pistoia
84. Potenza Province	Potenza
85. Ragusa Province	Ragusa
86. Ravenna Province	Ravenna
87. Reggio di Calabria Province	Reggio di Calabria
88. Reggio nell'Emilia Province	Reggio nell'Emilia
89. Rieti Province	Rieti
90. Roma Province	Roma
91. Rovigo Province	Rovigo
92. Salermo Province	Salermo
93. Sassari Province	Sassari
94. Savona Province	Savona
95. Siena Province	Siena
96. Siracusa Province	Siracusa
97. Sondrio Province	Sondrio
98. Teramo Province	Teramo
99. Terni Province	Terni
100. Torino Province	Torino
101. Trapani Province	Trapani
102. Trento Province	Trento
103. Treviso Province	Treviso
104. Trieste Province	Trieste
105. Varese Province	Varese
106. Venezia Province	Venezia
107. Vercelli Province	Vercelli
108. Verona Province	Verona
109. Vicenza Province	Vicenza
110. Viterbo Province	Viterbo

Ivory Coast (popular name)

The Republic of The Ivory Coast (official name)

'République du Côte d'Ivoire" (native name)

Abidjan (national capital)

Ivory Coast is located in Western Africa. It is bounded by
the Gulf of Guinea on the south; by Ghana on the east; by
Guinea and Liberia on the west; and by Mali and Upper
Volta on the north.

The Major Administrative Divisions are the 6 Departments.

The minor administrative divisions are the 108 subprefectures,
the 3 full and the 6 semi-administrative communes.

Departments	Capitals of Departments
1. Northern	Korhogo
2. West Central	Doala
3. Central	Bouaké
4. Southern	Abidjan
5. Western	Man
6. Eastern	Abengourou

Jamaica (popular name)

The Government of Jamaica (official name)

Kingston (national capital)

Jamaica is located in Southeastern North America. It is the
largest of the West Indies islands, in the Caribbean Sea,
just south of Cuba.

The Major Administrative Divisions of Jamaica number 13:
the 12 Parishes and the one City Corporation.

Major Administrative Div.	Capitals of Major Adm. Div.
1. St. Thomas Parish	Morant Bay
2. Portland Parish	Port Antonio
3. St. Mary Parish	Port Maria
4. St. Ann Parish	St. Anne Bay
5. Trelawney Parish	Falmouth
6. St. James Parish	Montego Bay
7. Hanover Parish	Lucea
8. Westmorland Parish	Savannah-la-Mar
9. St. Elizabeth Parish	Black River
10. Manchester Parish	Mandeville
11. Clarendon Parish	May Pen
12. St. Catherine Parish	Spanish Town
13. The City Corporation of Kingston and St. Andrew	Kingston

Japan (popular name)

The Japanese Government (official name)

"Nippon" (native name)

Tokyo (national capital)

Japan is located in Eastern Asia. Japan's islands are
bounded by the Sea of Japan on the west; by the Pacific
Ocean on the south and east; and by the U. S. S. R's Sak-
halin Island toward the north.

The Major Administrative Divisions of Japan number 46:
the 42 Prefectures or "ken," the 2 Special Cities or "fu;"
Hokkaido "Do;" and Tokyo "To."

The minor administrative divisions of Japan are the urban
counties or "shi" and the municipalities or "ku."

Major Administrative Div.	Capitals of Major Adm. Div.
1. Hiroshima Prefecture	Hiroshima
2. Okayama Prefecture	Okayama
3. Shimane Prefecture	Matsue
4. Tottori Prefecture	Tottori
5. Yamaguchi Prefecture	Yamaguchi
6. Fukui Prefecture	Fukui
7. Ishikawa Prefecture	Ishikawa
8. Niigata Prefecture	Niigata
9. Toyama Prefecture	Toyama
10. Chiba Prefecture	Chiba
11. Gunma Prefecture	Maebashi
12. Ibaraki Prefecture	Mito
13. Kanagawa Prefecture	Yokohama
14. Saitama Prefecture	Saitama
15. Tochigi Prefecture	Utsunomiya
16. Hyogo Prefecture	Himeji
17. Nara Prefecture	Nara
18. Shiga Prefecture	Otsu
19. Wakayama Prefecture	Wakayama
20. Fukuoka Prefecture	Fukuoka
21. Kagoshima Prefecture	Kagoshima
22. Kumamoto Prefecture	Kumamoto
23. Miyazaki Prefecture	Miyazaki
24. Nagasaki Prefecture	Nagasaki
25. Oita Prefecture	Oita
26. Saga Prefecture	Saga

27.	Ehime Prefecture	Matsuyama
28.	Kagawa Prefecture	Takamatsu
29.	Kochi Prefecture	Kochi
30.	Tokushima Prefecture	Tokushima
31.	Akita Prefecture	Akita
32.	Aomori Prefecture	Aomori
33.	Fukushima Prefecture	Fukushima
34.	Iwate Prefecture	Morioka
35.	Miyagi Prefecture	Sendai
36.	Yamagata Prefecture	Yamagata
37.	Aichi Prefecture	Nagoya
38.	Mie Prefecture	Tsu
39.	Shizuoka Prefecture	Shizuoka
40.	Gifu Prefecture	Gifu
41.	Nagano Prefecture	Nagano
42.	Yamanashi Prefecture	Kofu
43.	Osaka "Fu"	Osaka
44.	Kyoto "Fu"	Kyoto
45.	Hokkaido "Do"	Supporo
46.	Tokyo "To"	Tokyo

Jordan (popular name)

The Hashemite Kingdom of Jordan (official name)

"Al-Mamlakah Al-Hashimiyah Al Urdiniyah" (native name)

Amman (national capital)

Jordan is located in Western Asia, in the "Middle East" region.
It is bounded by Syria on the north; by Iraq on the east; by
Saudi Arabia on the southwest and south; and by Israel on the
west.

The Major Administrative Divisions of Jordan number 11:
the 10 governorates (or "aliya") and the one desert area.

The minor administrative divisions are the districts or
"aqdiya" and the subdistricts or "nawahin."

Major Administrative Div.	Capitals of Major Adm. Div.
1. Jerusalem Governorate	Jerusalem
2. Amman Governorate	Amman
3. Kerak Governorate	Kerak
4. Ma'an Governorate	Ma'an
5. Nablus Governorate	Nablus
6. Hebron Governorate	Hebron
7. Jenin Governorate	Jenin
8. Zarqa Governorate	Zarqa
9. 'Ajlun Governorate	Irbid
10. Balqa Governorate	Salt
11. The Desert Area	(Amman)

73

Kenya (popular name)

The Republic of Kenya (official name)

Nairobi (national capital)

Kenya is located in Eastern Africa. It is bounded by Somalia
on the northeast; by Ethiopia on the north; by Uganda on
the west; and by Tanzania on the south.

The Major Administrative Divisions of Kenya number 8: the
7 Administrative Regions and the one Federal Area.

The minor administrative districts of Kenya are the districts.

Major Administrative Div.	Capitals of Major Adm. Div.
1. North-Eastern Region	Wajir
2. Eastern Region	Embu
3. Central Region	Nairobi
4. Western Region	Bungoma
5. Coast Region	Mombassa
6. Nyanza Region	Kisumu
7. Rift Valley Region	Nakuru
8. The Federal Area	Nairobi

(Korea) North Korea (popular name)

The Democratic People's Republic of Korea (official name)

"Chosen Minchu-Chui Inmin Konghwa-Guk" (native name)

Pyongyang (national capital)

North Korea is located in Northeastern Asia. It is bounded
by China on the north; by the Sea of Japan on the east;
by South Korea on the south; and by the Yellow Sea on
the west.

The Major Administrative Divisions of North Korea are the
11 administrative divisions named variously as follows:
"si;" "do;" "pukto;" "namdo," and "chigu."

The minor administrative divisions are the countires and urban centers named variously as follows: "si;" "gun;"
"kun;" and "kuyok."

Administrative Divisions	Capitals of Adm. Div.
1. P'yongan-namdo	Namp'o
2. P'yongyang-si	Pyongyang City
3. Chagang-do	Kanggye
4. P'yongan-Pukto	Sinuiji
5. Yanggang-do	Hyesan
6. Hamgyong-pukto	Ch'ongjin
7. Hamgyong-namdo	Hamheung
8. Hwanghae-namdo	Haeju
9. Hwanghae-pukto	Sariwon
10. Kangwon-do	Wonson
11. Kaesong-Chigu	Kaesong City

(Korea) South Korea (popular name)

The Republic of Korea (official name)

'Daehan-Minkuk" (native name)

Seoul (national capital)

South Korea is located in Northeastern Asia. It is bounded
by North Korea on the north; by the Yellow Sea on the
west; by the Korean Straights on the south; and by the
Sea of Japan on the east.

The Major Administrative Divisions of South Korea number
11: the 9 Provinces and the 2 Special Cities.

The minor administrative divisions of South Korea are the
139 counties or 'kun," the 30 cities, and numerous subdivisions called variously: 'myun," 'eup," 'ri," 'tong,"
and 'pang."

Major Administrative Div.	Capitals of Major Adm. Div.
1. Kyunggi-do Province	Suwon
2. Kangwon-do Province	Chunchon
3. Chungchong-Pukto Province	Chongju
4. Chungchong-Namdo Province	Taejon
5. Cholla-Pukto Province	Chonju
6. Cholla-Namdo Province	Kwangju
7. Kyungsang-Pukto Province	Taegu
8. Kyungsang–Namdo Province	Pusan
9. Cheju-do Province	Cheju
10. Pusan Special City	Pusan
11. Seoul Special City	Seoul

Kuwait (popular name)

The State of Kuwait (official name)

"Dauwlat Al-Kuwayt" (native name)

Kuwait City (national capital)

Kuwait is located in Southwestern Asia, in the northeastern corner of the Arabian Peninsula. It is bounded by the Persian Gulf on the east; by the Kuwaiti-Saudi Arabian Neutral Zone and Saudi Arabia on the south; and by Iraq on the west and the north.

The Major Administrative Divisions of Kuwait are the 3 Provincial Governorates.

Provincial Governorates	Capitals of Prov. Govern.
1. Kuwait	Kuwait
2. Ahmadi	Ahmadi
3. Howalli	Howalli

Laos (popular name)

The Kingdom of Laos (official name)

"Royaume de Laos" (native name)

Vientiane (national capital)

Laos is located in Southeastern Asia. It is bounded by Mainland China on the north; by North Vietnam and South Vietnam on the east; by Cambodia on the south; and by Thailand and Burma on the west.

The Major Administrative Divisions of Laos are the 14 Provinces or "khoveng."

The minor administrative divisions of Laos are the 78 districts or "muongs," the many townships or "tasseng," and the villages or "ban."

Provinces	Provincial Capitals
1. Phong Saly	Phong Saly
2. Houa Khong	Nam Tha
3. Luang Prabang	Luang Prabang
4. Sayaboury	Sayaboury
5. Vientiane	Vientiane

6.	Sam Neua	Sam Neua
7.	Xieng Khouang	Xieng Khouang
8.	Khammoung	Thakhek
9.	Savannakhet	Savannakhet
10.	Saravane	Saravane
11.	Attopeu	Muong May
12.	Bassac	Pakse
13.	Borikane	Paksane
14.	Sithandone	Kong

Lebanon (popular name)

The Republic of Lebanon (official name)

"Al-Jumhuriyah al-Lubnaniyah" (native name)

Beirut (national capital)

Lebanon is located in Southwestern Asia, in the area known as the "Middle East." It is bounded by Syria on the north and east; by Israel on the south; and by the Mediterranean Sea on the west.

The Major Administrative Divisions of Lebanon are the 5 Circumscriptions or "mohafazets."

Circumscriptions	Capitals of Circumscriptions
1. Beirut	Beirut
2. Lebanon North	Tripoli
3. Lebanon South	Sidon
4. Mount Libanus	Baabda
5. El Begaa	Zahleh

Liberia (popular name)

The Republic of Liberia (official name)

Monrovia (national capital)

Liberia is located in Southwestern Africa. It is bounded by Sierra Leone on the west; by Guinea on the north; by the Ivory Coast on the east; and by the Atlantic Ocean on the south and southwest.

The Major Administrative Divisions of Liberia are the 9 Counties.

The minor administrative divisions of Liberia are the dis-

Liberia (continued)

tricts and the chiefdoms.

Counties	County Capitals
1. Grand Bassa	Buchanan
2. Cape Mount	Robertsport
3. Maryland	Harper
4. Montserrado	Monrovia
5. Sinoe	Greenville
6. Grand Gedeh	Tchien
7. Nimba	Saniquellie
8. Bong	Gbanga
9. Loffa	Voinjama

Libya (popular name)

The Kingdom of Libya (official name)

"Al Mamlaka al Libiyya al Muttahida" (native name)

El Beida (national capital)

Libya is located in Northern Africa. It is bounded by the Mediterranean Sea on the north; by Egypt and Sudan on the east; by Tunisia and Algeria on the west; and by Sudan, Chad, and Niger on the south.

The Major Administrative Divisions of Libya are the 3 Provinces.

The minor administrative divisions of Libya are the administrative districts.

Provinces	Provincial Capitals
1. Barqah	Benghazi
2. Fezzan	Sabbah
3. Tripolitania	Tripoli

Note: Recent reports speak of a proposed new administrative arrangement which divides Libya into 10 commissioner's districts, each governed by a "muhafidh."

Liechtenstein (popular name)

The Principality of Liechtenstein (official name)

"Fürstentum Liechtenstein" (native name)

Vaduz (national capital)

Liechtenstein is located in Northwestern Europe. It is
bounded by Austria on the north and east; and by Switzerland on the south and west.

The Major Administrative Divisions of Liechtenstein are the
11 Communities or "gemeinden."

Communities	Capitals of Communities
1. Vaduz	Vaduz
2. Triesen	Triesen
3. Balzers	Balzers
4. Triesenberg	Triesenberg
5. Schaan	Schaan
6. Planken	Planken
7. Eschen	Eschen
8. Mavren	Mavren
9. Gamprion	Gamprion
10. Ruggell	Ruggell
11. Schellenberg	Schellenberg

Luxembourg (popular name)

The Grand Duchy of Luxembourg (official name)

"Grand-Duché de Luxembourg" (native name)

Luxembourg (national capital)

Luxembourg is located in Northwestern Europe. It is
bounded by West Germany on the east; by France on the
south; and by Belgium on the west and north.

The Major Administrative Divisions of Luxembourg number
15:   the 3 Districts and the 15 Cantons.

Major Administrative Div.	Capitals of Major Adm. Div.
1. Luxembourg District	Luxembourg
2. Diekirch District	Diekirch
3. Gravenmacher District	Gravenmacher
4. Capellen Canton	Capellen
5. Esch-sur-Alzette Canton	Esch-sur-Alzette
6. Luxembourg Canton	Luxembourg
7. Mersch Canton	Mersch

Luxembourg (continued)

Major Administrative Div.	Capitals of Major Adm. Div.
8. Clervaux Canton	Clervaux
9. Diekirch Canton	Diekirch
10. Rédange Canton	Rédange
11. Vianden Canton	Vianden
12. Wiltz Canton	Wiltz
13. Gravenmacher Canton	Gravenmacher
14. Echternach Canton	Echternach
15. Remich Canton	Remich

Malagasy (popular name)

The Malagasy Republic (official name)

"Repoblika Malagasy" (native name)

Tananarive (national capital)

Malagasy is located off the east coast of Southern Africa. It is an island republic bounded by the Indian Ocean on all sides, and facing Mozambique to the west.

The Major Administrative Divisions of Malagasy number 24: the 6 Provinces and the 18 Prefectures.

The minor administrative divisions of Malagasy are the 91 sub-prefectures or "sous-préfectures," and the cantons and communes.

Major Administrative Div.	Capitals of Major Adm. Div.
1. Fianarantsoa Province	Fianarantsoa
2. Majunga Province	Majunga
3. Tamatave Province	Tamatave
4. Diégo-Suarez Province	Diégo-Suarez
5. Tuléar Province	Tuléar
6. Tananarive Province	Tananarive
7. Délégation Générale Prefecture	Tananarive
8. Vakinankaratra à Antsirabé Pref.	Ansirabé
9. Itasy à Miarinarivo Prefecture	Miarinarivo
10. Fianarantsoa Prefecture	Fianarantsoa
11. Mananjary Prefecture	Mananjary
12. Farafangana Prefecture	Farafangana
13. Tamatave Prefecture	Tamatave
14. Ambatondrazaka Prefecture	Ambatondrazaka
15. Fénérive Prefecture	Fénérive

16. Majunga Prefecture	Majunga
17. Antsohy Prefecture	Antsohy
18. Maintirano Prefecture	Maintirano
19. Tuléar Prefecture	Tuléar
20. Fort Dauphin Prefecture	Fort Dauphin
21. Morondava Prefecture	Morondava
22. Diégo-Suarez Prefecture	Diégo-Suarez
23. Antalaha Prefecture	Antalaha
24. Nossi-Bé Prefecture	Nossi-Bé

Malawi (popular name)

The Government of Malawi (official name)

Zomba (national capital)

Malawi is located in South-central Africa. It is bounded by Tanzania on the north; by Tanzania and Mozambique on the east and south; and by Zambia on the west.

The Major Administrative Divisions of Malawi number 26: the 3 Regions and the 23 Districts.

The minor administrative divisions of Malawi are the 132 local councils.

Major Administrative Div.	Capitals of Major Adm. Div.
1. Northern Region	Mzuzu
2. Central Region	Lilongwe
3. Southern Region	Blantyre
4. Blantyre District	Blantyre
5. Chikwawa District	Chikwawa
6. Chitipa District	Chitipa
7. Chiradzulu District	Chiradzulu
8. Cholo District	Cholo
9. Dedza District	Dedza
10. Dowa District	Dowa
11. Fort Johnston District	Fort Johnston
12. Kasupe District	Kasupe
13. Lilongwe District	Lilongwe
14. Karonga District	Karonga
15. Nkhotakota District	Nkhotakota
16. Nsanje District	Nsanje
17. Zomba District	Zomba
18. Mlanje District	Mlanje
19. Mzimba District	Mzimba
20. Ncheu District	Ncheu

Malawi (continued)

Major Administrative Div.	Capitals of Major Adm. Div.
21. Rumpi District	Rumpi
22. Salima District	Salima
23. Mchinji District	Mchinji
24. Ntchisi District	Ntchisi
25. Kasungu District	Kasungu
26. Nkhata Bay District	Nkhata

Malaysia (popular name)

The Federation of Malaysia (official name)

"Persekutuan Tanah Melaya" (native name)

Kuala Lumpur (national capital)

Malaysia is located in Southeastern Asia. It occupies the northern part of Borneo and the southern part of the Malay Peninsula; it is bounded by Thailand on the north; by the China Sea on the east and south; by Sumatra on the southwest; and by the Straights of Malacca and the Bay of Bengal on the west.

The Major Administrative Divisions of Malaysia are the 13 States.

The minor administrative divisions of Malaysia are the districts.

States	State Capitals
1. Sarawak	Kuching
2. Sabah	Jesselton
3. Kedah	Alor Star
4. Perlis	Kangar
5. Malacca	Malacca
6. Penang	George Town
7. Perak	Ipoh
8. Selangor	Kuala Lumpur
9. Negri Sembilan	Seremban
10. Johore	Johore Bahru
11. Pahang	Kuantan
12. Trengganu	Kuala Trengganu
13. Kelantan	Kota Bahru

Maldive Islands (popular name)

The Kingdom of the Maldive Islands (official name)

"Divehi Raje" (native name)

Malé (national capital)

The Maldive Islands are an island nation located in Southern
Asia.   They lie to the southwest of Ceylon in the Indian
Ocean.

The Maldive Islands are administratively divided into 17
Provinces or "atolu."

Provinces
1. Ihavandiffulu
2. Tiladummati
3. Malcolm
4. Miladummadulu
5. Fadiffolu
6. North Malosmadulu
7. South Malosmadulu
8. Horsburgh
9. Malé
10. South Malé
11. Ari
12. Felidu
13. Mulaku
14. Nilandu
15. Kolumadulu
16. Suvadiva
17. Haddummati

Mali (popular name)

The Republic of Mali (official name)

Bamako (national capital)

Mali is located in Western Africa.

Mali is bounded by Algeria on the north; by Niger on the
east and southeast; by Upper Volta and Ivory Coast on the
south; and by Guinea and Senegal on the west.

The Major Administrative Divisions of Mali are the 6 Regional Governments.

Mali (continued)

The minor administrative divisions of Mali are the 42 districts or "cercles."

Regional Governments	Capitals of Regional Govts.
1. Kayes	Kayes
2. Bamako	Bamako
3. Ségou	Ségou
4. Sikasso	Sikasso
5. Mopti	Mopti
6. Gao	Gao

Malta (popular name)

The Government of Malta (official name)

Valletta (national capital)

Malta is an island nation located in Southern Europe, in the Mediterranean due south of Sicily.

Malta has but 2 Administrative Divisions:
1. The Maltese Central Administration, with its capital in Valletta
2. The Gozo Civic Council, with its capital in Victoria.

Mauritania (popular name)

The Islamic Republic of Mauritania (official name)

"République Islamique de Mauritanie" (native name)

Nouakchott (national capital)

Mauritania is located in Western Africa. It is bounded by the Atlantic Ocean and Spanish Rio de Oro on the west; by Algeria on the north and northeast; by Mali on the east; and by Senegal on the south.

The Major Administrative Divisions of Mauritania are the 12 "Cercles."

The minor administrative divisions of Mauritania are the 16 "subdivisions."

Cercles	Capitals of Cercles
1. Assaba	Kiffa

2.	Brakna	Aleg
3.	Gorgol	Kaedi
4.	Guidimaka	Selibaby
5.	Adrar	Atar
6.	Inchiri	Akjoujt
7.	Trarza	Rosso
8.	Tagant	Tidjikja
9.	Hodh Occidental	Aioun
10.	Hodh Oriental	Nema
11.	Baie du Levrier	Port-Etienne
12.	Tiris Zemmour	Fort-Gouraud

Mexico (popular name)

The United Mexican States (official name)

"Estados Unidos Mexicanos" (native name)

Mexico City (national capital)

Mexico is located in the Southern part of North America. It is bounded by the United States on the north; by the Gulf of Mexico, the Caribbean Sea, and British Honduras on the east; by the Pacific Ocean and Guatemala on the south; and by the Pacific Ocean on the west.

The Major Administrative Divisions of Mexico number 32: the 29 States; the 2 Federal Territories; and the one Federal District.

The minor administrative divisions of Mexico are the districts and local municipalities.

Major Administrative Div.	Capitals of Major Adm. Div.
1. Aguacalientes State	Aguacalientes
2. Baja California State	Mexicali
3. Campeche State	Campeche
4. Chiapas State	Tuxtla Gutierrez
5. Chihuahua State	Chihuahua
6. Coahuila State	Saltillo
7. Colima State	Colima
8. Durango State	Durango
9. Guanajuato State	Guanajuato
10. Guerrero State	Chilpancingo
11. Hidalgo State	Pachuca
12. Jalisco State	Guadalajara
13. Mexico State	Toluca
14. Michoacan State	Morelia

85

Mexico (continued)

Major Administrative Div.	Capitals of Major Adm. Div.
15. Morelas State	Cueravaca
16. Nayarit State	Tepic
17. Nueva Leon State	Monterrey
18. Oaxaca State	Oaxaca
19. Quaretaro State	Quaretaro
20. San Luis Potosi State	San Luis Potosi
21. Sinaloa State	Culiacan
22. Sinora State	Hermorillo
23. Puebla State	Puebla
24. Tabisco State	Villa Hermosa
25. Tamaulipas State	Ciudad Victoria
26. Tlaxcala State	Tlaxcala
27. Veracruz State	Jalapa Enriquez
28. Yucatan State	Merida
29. Zacatecas State	Zacatecas
30. Baja California Sur Territory	La Paz
31. Quintano Roo Territory	Ciudad Chetumal
32. "Distrito Federal"	Mexico City

Monaco (popular name)

The Principality of Monaco (official name)

"Principauté de Monaco" (native name)

Monaco City (national capital)

Monaco is located in Northwestern Europe. It is a very
small principality on the Mediterranean Sea surrounded on
all but the sea side by France's Département de Alps
Maritimes.

Monaco has but one administrative commune called "La Con-
seil Communal." This commune incorporates the three
former municipalities of Monaco-Ville, La Condamine,
and Monte Carlo.

Mongolia (popular name)

The Mongolian People's Republic (official name)

"Bughut Nairamdakh Mongol Arat Ulus" (native name)

Ulan Bator (national capital)

Mongolia is located in Northeastern Asia. It is bounded by
the U.S.S.R. on the north; by Mainland China on the east
and south; and the U.S.S.R.'s Turkestan on the west.

The Major Administrative Divisions of Mongolia number 19:
the 17 Provinces or "aimak," and the 2 Independent Cities.

The minor administrative divisions are the 404 counties or
"somon" and the 27 urban districts or "khoren."

Major Administrative Div.	Capitals of Major Adm. Div.
1. Ara-Khangai Province	Tsetserlik
2. Bayan-Ulegei Province	Ulgi
3. Bayan-Khongor Province	Bayan-Khongor
4. Bulgan Province	Bulgan
5. Gobi-Altai Province	Yeson-Bulag
6. East Gobi Province	Sain-Shand
7. Central Gobi	Mandal-Gobi
8. Dzabkhan Province	Zhavkhlante
9. Ubur-Khangai Province	Arvai-Khar
10. South Gobi	Dalan-Zadgad
11. Central Province	Zun-Mud
12. Sukhe-Bator Province	Barun-Urt
13. Ubsa-Nor Province	Ulan-Gom
14. Khubsugul Province	Murun
15. Kentai Province	Undurkhan
16. Choibalsan Province	Choibalsan
17. Kobdo Province	Dhurgalantu
18. Ulan Bator Independent City	
19. Sukhe-Bator Independent City	

Morocco (popular name)

The Kingdom of Morocco (official name)

"Al-Mamlaka al-Maghrebia" (native name)

Rabat (national capital)

Morocco is located in Northwest Africa. It is bounded by
Algeria on the east; by the Mediterranean Sea on the
North; by the Atlantic Ocean on the west; and by Spanish
Rio de Oro and Algeria on the south.

The Major Administrative Divisions of Morocco number 16:
the 14 Provinces and the 2 Urban Prefectures.

87

Morocco (continued)

The minor administrative divisions of Morocco are the 72 "cercles;" the 286 districts or "caidats;" and the some 800 communes.

Major Administrative Div.	Capitals of Major Adm. Div.
1. Agadir Province	Agadir
2. Casablanca Province	Casablanca
3. Fès Province	Fès
4. Marrakech Province	Marrakech
5. Meknes Province	Meknes
6. Ouerzazat Province	Ouerzazat
7. Oujda Province	Oujda
8. Rabat Province	Kenitra
9. Safi Province	Safi
10. Tafilalet Province	Ksar Souk
11. Tanger Province	Tanger
12. Taza Province	Taza
13. Tarfaya Province	Tan-Tan
14. Tétouan Province	Tétouan
15. The City of Rabat Prefecture	
16. The City of Casablanca Prefecture	

Muscat and Oman (popular name)

The Sultanate of Muscat and Oman and Dependencies (official name)

"Sultanat Masqat wah 'Uman" (native name)

Muscat City (national capital)

Muscat and Oman is located in Southwestern Asia, on the Arabian Peninsula. It is bounded by the Gulf of Oman and The Trucial States on the north and northwest; by Saudi Arabia on the west; and by the Arabian Sea on the south and east.

Muscat and Oman's Administrative Divisions are the one capital municipality and the 8 regional governorates or 'walis:"

1. The Municipality of Muscat and Matrah
2. Ru'us al-Jibal Governorate
3. Batinah Governorate
4. Dhalhirah Governorate

5. Central Oman Governorate
6. al-Sharqiyah Governorate
7. Jala'n Governorate
8. Dhufar Governorate
9. Shumailiyah Governorate

Nepal (popular name)

The Kingdom of Nepal (official name)

Kathmandu (national capital)

Nepal is located in Southern Asia. It is bounded by Tibet on the north; and by India on the east, south, and west.

The Major Administrative Divisions of Nepal are the 14 Zones.

The minor administrative divisions of Nepal are the 75 "zillas" or administrative districts.

Zones	Capitals of Zones
1. Mechi	Ilam
2. Kosi	Biratnagar
3. Sagarmatha	Rajbiraj
4. Janakpur	Jaleswar
5. Bagmati	Kathmandu
6. Narayani	Bhimphedi
7. Gandaki	Pokhara
8. Lumbini	Bhairawa
9. Dhaulagiri	Baglung
10. Rapati	Sallyan
11. Karnali	Jumla
12. Bheri	Nepalganj
13. Seti	Dhangarhi
14. Mahakali	Dandeldhura

Netherlands, The (popular name)

The Kingdom of the Netherlands (official name)

"Koninkrijk Der Nederlanden" (native name)

Amsterdam (national capital)

The Netherlands is located in Northwestern Europe. It is bounded by West Germany on the east; by Belgium on the south; and by the North Sea on the west and the north.

The Netherlands (continued)

The Major Administrative Divisions of the Netherlands number 15: the 11 Provinces, the 2 Reclaimed Territories or "polders," and the 2 Overseas Territories.

The minor administrative divisions of The Netherlands are the over 1000 municipalities or "gemeente."

Major Administrative Div.	Capitals of Major Adm. Div.
1. Drente Province	Assen
2. Friesland Province	Leeuwarden
3. Gelderland Province	Arnhem
4. Groningen Province	Groningen
5. Limburg Province	Maastricht
6. Noord-Brabant Province	's-Hertogenbosch
7. Noord-Holland Province	Amsterdam
8. Overijssel Province	Zwolle
9. Utrecht Province	Utrecht
10. Zeeland Province	Middleburg
11. Zuid-Holland Province	's-Gravenhage
12. North-East Polder	Emmeloord
13. Eastern Flevoland Polder	Lelystad
14. Surinam Overseas Territory	Paramaribo
15. Netherlands Antilles Territory	Willemstad

Further notes on the administrative divisions of the Overseas Territories.

Surinam is divided into 7 districts

Districts	District Capitals
1. Paramaribo	Paramaribo
2. Suriname	Paramaribo
3. Commewijne	Nieuw Amsterdam
4. Saramacca	Groningen
5. Kickerie	Nieuw Nickerie
6. Coronie	Totness
7. Marowijne	Albina

The Netherlands Antilles is divided into 6 districts

Districts	District Capitals
1. Curaçao	Willemstad
2. Aruba	Oranjestad
3. Bonaire	Kralendijk
4. St. Martin	Phillipsburg
5. St. Eustatius	Oranjestad
6. Saba	The Bottom

New Zealand (popular name)

The Government of New Zealand (official name)

Wellington (national capital)

New Zealand is located in the South Pacific Ocean, southeast of Australia, and separated from Australia by the
Tasman Sea.

The Major Administrative Divisions of New Zealand number
134: the 116 County Council, and the 18 City Councils.

The minor administrative divisions of New Zealand are the
127 borough councils.

Major Administrative Div.	Capitals of Major Adm. Div.
1. Akaroa County Council	Duvauchelle
2. Akitio County Council	Pongaroa
3. Amuri County Council	Culverden
4. Ashburton County Council	Ashburton
5. Ashley County Council	Loburn
6. Awatere County Council	Seddon
7. Bay of Islands County Council	Kawakawa
8. Bruce County Council	Milton
9. Buller County Council	Westport
10. Chatham Is. County Council	Waitangi, Chatham Is.
11. Cheviot County Council	Cheviot
12. Clifton County Council	Waitara
13. Clutha County Council	Balclutha
14. Cook County Council	Gisborne
15. Coromandel County Council	Coromandel
16. Dannevirke County Council	Dannevirke
17. Egmont County Council	Opunake
18. Eketahuna County Council	Eketahuna
19. Ellesmere County Council	Leeston
20. Eltham County Council	Eltham
21. Eyre County Council	Kaiapoi
22. Featherston County Council	Martinborough
23. Franklin County Council	Pukekohe
24. Geraldine County Council	Geraldine
25. Golden Bay County Council	Takaha
26. Great Barrier Is. County Counc.	Auck
27. Grey County Council	Greymouth
28. Haiswell County Council	Haiswell
29. Hauraki Plains County Council	Ngatea
30. Hawera County Council	Hawera

New Zealand (continued)

Major Administrative Div.	Capitals of Major Adm. Div.
31. Hawke's Bay County Coun.	Napier
32. Heathcote County Council	Christchurch
33. Hobson County Council	Dargaville
34. Hokianga County Council	Rawene
35. Horowhenua County Council	Levin
36. Hutt County Council	Wellington
37. Inangahua County Council	Reefton
38. Inglewood County Council	Inglewood
39. Kaikoura County Council	Kaikoura
40. Kairanga County Council	Palmerston N.
41. Kiwitea County Council	Kimbolton
42. Kowal County Council	Rangiora
43. Lake County Council	Queenstown
44. Levels County Council	Timaru
45. Mackenzie County Council	Fairlie
46. Malvern County Council	Darfield
47. Manawatu County Council	Sanson
48. Mangonui County Council	Kaitaia
49. Maniototo County Council	Ranfurly
50. Manukau County Council	Auckland
51. Marlborough County Council	Blenheim
52. Masterton County Council	Masterton
53. Matakaoa County Council	Te Araroa
54. Matamata County Council	Tirau
55. Mauriceville County Council	Masterton
56. Mount Herbert County Council	Christchurch
57. Murchison County Council	Murchison
58. Ohinemuri County Council	Pacroa
59. Opotiki County Council	Opotiki
60. Oroua County Council	Feilding
61. Otamatea County Council	Paparoa
62. Otorohanga County Council	Otorohanga
63. Oxford County Council	Oxford
64. Pahiatua County Council	Pahiatua
65. Paparua County Council	Chch. 4
66. Patangaia County Council	Waipukurau
67. Patea County Council	Patea
68. Peninsula County Council	Portobello
69. Piako County Council	Te Aroha
70. Pohangina County Council	Ashhurst
71. Raglan County Council	Ngaruawahia
72. Rangiora County Council	Rangiora
73. Rangiokei County Council	Marton
74. Rodney County Council	Warkworth

75.	Rotorua County Council	Rotorua
76.	Southland County Council	Invercargill
77.	Stewart Island County Council	Halfmoon Bay, Stewart Is.
78.	Stratford County Council	Stratford
79.	Taieri County Council	Mosgiel
80.	Taranaki County Council	New Plymouth
81.	Taumarunui County Council	Taumarunui
82.	Taupo County Council	Taupo
83.	Tauranga County Council	Tauranga
84.	Tawera County Council	Christchurch
85.	Thames County Council	Thames
86.	Tuapeka County Council	Lawrence
87.	Uawa County Council	Tolaga Bay
88.	Vincent County Council	Clyde
89.	Walapu County Council	Te Puia Springs
90.	Waihemo County Council	Palmerston
91.	Waikato County Council	Hamilton E.
92.	Waikohu County Council	Te Karaka
93.	Waikouaiti County Council	Waikouaiti
94.	Waimairi County Council	Christchurch
95.	Waimarino County Council	Raetihi
96.	Waimate County Council	Waimate
97.	Waimate West County Council	Manaia
98.	Waimea County Council	Nelson
99.	Waipa County Council	Te Awamutu
100.	Waipara County Council	Waikari
101.	Waipawa County Council	Waipawa
102.	Waipukurau County Council	Waipukurau
103.	Wairarapa Sth. County Council	Carterton
104.	Wairewa County Council	Little River
105.	Wairora County Council	Wairoa
106.	Waitaki County Council	Oamaru
107.	Waitemata County Council	Auckland
108.	Waitomo County Council	Te Kuiti
109.	Waitotara County Council	Wanganui
110.	Wallace County Council	Otautau
111.	Wanganui County Council	Wanganui
112.	Westland County Council	Hokitika
113.	Whakatane County Council	Whakatane
114.	Whangarei County Council	Whangarei
115.	Whangaroa County Countil	Kaeo
116.	Woodville County Council	Woodville
117.	Auckland City Council	Auckland
118.	Christchurch City Council	Christchurch
119.	Dunedin City Council	Dunedin
120.	Gisborne City Council	Gisborne
121.	Hamilton City Council	Hamilton

New Zealand (continued)

Major Administrative Div.	Capitals of Major Adm. Div.
122. Hastings City Council	Hastings
123. Invercargill City Council	Invercargill
124. Lower Hutt City Council	Lower Hutt
125. Napier City Council	Napier
126. Nelson City Council	Nelson
127. New Plymouth City Council	New Plymouth
128. Palmerston North City Counc.	Palmerston North
129. Rotorua City Council	Rotorua
130. Takapuna City Council	Takapuna
131. Tauranga City Council	Tauranga
132. Timaru City Council	Timaru
133. Wanganui City Council	Wanganui
134. Wellington City Council	Wellington

Nicaragua (popular name)

The Republic of Nicaragua (official name)

"Republica de Nicaragua" (native name)

Managua (national capital)

Nicaragua is located in Southwestern North America, in the area commonly called "Central America." It is bounded by Honduras on the north; by the Caribbean Sea on the east; by Costa Rica on the south; and by the Pacific Ocean on the west.

The Major Administrative Divisions of Nicaragua number 17: the 16 Departments and the one National District.

The minor administrative divisions are the municipal boards.

Major Administrative Div.	Capitals of Major Adm. Div.
1. Boaco Department	Boaco
2. Carazo Department	Jinotepe
3. Chinandega Department	Chinandega
4. Esteli Department	Esteli
5. Ghontales Department	Juigalpa
6. Granada Department	Granada
7. Jinotega Department	Jinotega
8. Leon Department	Leon
9. Madriz Department	Somoto
10. Managua Department	Managua
11. Masaya Department	Masaya

94

12.	Matagalpa Department	Matagalpa
13.	Nueva Segovia Department	Ocotal
14.	Rio San Juan Department	San Carlos
15.	Rivas Department	Rivas
16.	Zelaya Department	Bluefields
17.	Comarca del Cabo Gracias a Dios National District	Cabo Gracias a Dios

Niger (popular name)

The Republic of Niger (official name)

"La République du Niger" (native name)

Niamey (national capital)

Niger is located in Western Africa. It is bounded by Libya and Algeria on the north; by Chad on the east; by Upper Volta, Dahomey, and Nigeria on the south; and by Mali on the west.

The Major Administrative Divisions of Niger number 43: the 16 Districts or "cercles;" and the 27 Subdistricts or "Circonscriptions."

The minor administrative divisions are the "administrative posts."

Major Administrative Div.	Capitals of Major Adm. Div.
1. Niamey District	Niamey
2. Agades District	Agades
3. Birni N'Konni District	Birni N'Konni
4. Dogondoutchi District	Dogondoutchi
5. Dosso District	Dosso
6. Filingue District	Filingue
7. Madsoua District	Madsoua
8. Magaria District	Magaria
9. Maradi District	Maradi
10. N'Guimi District	N'Guimi
11. Tahoua District	Tahoua
12. Tessaoua District	Tessaoua
13. Tillaberi District	Tillaberi
14. Goure District	Goure
15. Zinder District	Zinder
16. Tera District	Tera
17. Iférouane Subdistrict	Iférouane
18. Bilma Subdistrict	Bilma
19. N'Gourti Subdistrict	N'Guigmi

Niger (continued)

Major Administrative Div.	Capitals of Major Adm. Div.
20. Maine Soroa Subdistrict	Maine
21. Goure Subdistrict	Goure
22. Tanout Subdistrict	Tanout
23. Zinder Subdistrict	Zinder
24. Matameye Subdistrict	Matameye
25. Magaria Subdistrict	Magaria
26. Tessaoua Subdistrict	Tessaoua
27. Mayahi Subdistrict	Mayahi
28. Dakoro Subdistrict	Dakoro
29. Tchin Tabaraden Subdistrict	Tchin Tabaraden
30. Keita Subdistrict	Keita
31. Tahoua Subdistrict	Tahoua
32. Ilhela Subdistrict	Ilhela
33. Madsoua Subdistrict	Madsoua
34. Birni N'Konni	Birni N'Konni
35. Dogondoutchi Subdistrict	Dogondoutchi
36. Filingue Subdistrict	Filingue
37. Loga Subdistrict	Loga
38. Birni N'Gaoure Subdistrict	Dosso
39. Gaya Subdistrict	Gaya
40. Niamey Subdistrict	Niamey
41. Tera Subdistrict	Tera
42. Ouallam Subdistrict	Ouallam
43. Say Subdistrict	Say

Nigeria (popular name)

The Federal Republic of Nigeria (official name)

Lagos (national capital)

Nigeria is located in Western Africa. It is bounded by Niger on the north; by Chad on the northeast; by Cameroon on the east; by the Gulf of Guinea on the south; and by Dahomey on the west.

The Major Administrative Divisions of Nigeria number 5: the 4 Regions and the one Capital District.

The minor administrative divisions of Nigeria are the provinces and administrative districts.

Major Administrative Div.	Capitals of Major Adm. Div.
1. Western Nigeria Region	Ibadan

96

2. Eastern Nigeria Region	Enugu
3. Northern Nigeria Region	Kaduna
4. Midwest Nigeria Region	Benin
5. The Capital District	Lagos

Further note on the minor administrative divisions of Northern Nigeria. It is divided into 13 provinces:

1. Sokoto
2. Katsina
3. Kano
4. Bornu
5. Niger
6. Zaria
7. Plateau
8. Benue
9. Adamawa
10. Bauchi
11. Sardauna
12. Kabba
13. Ilorin

Norway (popular name)

The Kingdom of Norway (official name)

"Kongeriket Norge" (native name)

Oslo (national capital)

Norway is located in Northwestern Europe, on the Scandinavian Peninsula. It is bounded by the Berents Sea on the north; by Sweden, Finland, and the U.S.S.R. on the east; by the North Sea on the south; and by the Atlantic Ocean and the Norwegian Sea on the west.

The Major Administrative Divisions of Norway number 25: the 20 Counties or "fylker;" the 2 Territories; and the 3 Dependencies.

The minor administrative divisions of Norway are the 466 urban and rural municipalities or "herad," and the 1029 parishes or "sogn."

Major Administrative Div.	Capitals of Major Adm. Div.
1. Akershus County	Baerhum
2. Aust-Agder County	Arondal
3. Buskerud County	Drammen
4. Finnmark County	Vadsø

97

Norway (continued)

Major Administrative Div.	Capitals of Major Adm. Div.
5. Hedmark County	Hamar
6. Hordaland County	Voss
7. Möre og Romsdal County	Moldo
8. Nordland County	Bodø
9. Nord-Tröndelag County	Steinkjor
10. Oppland County	Lillehammer
11. Østfold County	Moss
12. Rogaland County	Stavanger
13. Sogn og Fjordane County	Hermansverk
14. Sör-Tröndelag County	Trondheim
15. Telemark County	Skien
16. Troms	Tromsø
17. Vest-Agder County	Kristiansand
18. Vestfold County	Tøonsberg
19. Oslo County	Oslo
20. Bergen County	Bergen
21. Svalbard Territory	Green Harbor
22. Jan Mayen Territory	Jameson Bay
23. Bouvet Island Dependency	
24. Peter Island Dependency	
25. The Norwegian Antarctic Dependency	

Pakistan (popular name)

The Islamic Republic of Pakistan (official name)

Rawalpindi (provisional national capital).   In the planning
stage is the new permanent capital city of "Islamabad."

Pakistan is located in South Asia, and it occupies two zones
of the Indian subcontinent.

West Pakistan is bounded by Iran and Afghanistan on the
west and northwest; by India on the southeast; by the
Arabian Sea on the south; and by India on the northeast.

East Pakistan is bounded by India on the east, west and
north; by Burma on the east; and by the Bay of Bengal
on the south.

The Major Administrative Divisions of Pakistan number 19:
the 2 Governor's Provinces; the 3 Semi-Autonomous
Areas; the 13 Commissioner's Divisions; and the Azad
Kahmir.

The minor administrative divisions of Pakistan are called agencies and districts.

Major Administrative Div.	Capitals of Major Adm. Div.
1. West Pakistan Province	Lahore
2. East Pakistan Province	Dacca
3. Swat Area	Saidu
4. Dir Area	Dir
5. Chitral Area	Chitral
6. Peshawar Division	Peshawar
7. Dera Ismail Khaa Division	Dera Ismail Khaa
8. Rawalpindi Division	Rawalpindi
9. Lahore Division	Lahore
10. Multan Division	Multan
11. Bahawalpur Division	Bahawalpur
12. Khairpur Division	Khairpur
13. Hyderabad Division	Hyderabad
14. Quetta Division	Quetta
15. Kalat Division	Kalat
16. Dacca Division	Dacca
17. Chittagong Division	Chittagong
18. Rajshahi Division	Rajshahi
19. The Azad Kashmir	Muzaffarabad

Panama (popular name)

The Republic of Panama (official name)

"Republica de Panama" (native name)

Panama City (national capital)

Panama is located in Southernmost North America, in the area of "Central America." It is bounded by Colombia on the east and south; by Costa Rica on the west and north; and is bisected by the United States Canal Zone.

The Major Administrative Divisions of Panama are the 9 Provinces.

The minor administrative divisions of Panama are the municipal districts.

Provinces	Provincial Capitals
1. Bocas del Toro	Bocas del Toro
2. Chiriqui	David
3. Cocle	Penonomé

Panama (continued)

Provinces	Provincial Capitals
4. Colon	Colon
5. Darien	La Palma
6. Herrera	Chitré
7. Los Santos	Las Tablas
8. Panama	Panama City
9. Veraguas	Santiago

Paraguay (popular name)

The Republic of Paraguay (official name)

"Republica del Paraguay" (native name)

Asunción (national capital)

Paraguay is located in Central South America. It is bounded by Bolivia and Brazil on the north; by Brazil and Argentina on the east; by Argentina on the south; and by Argentina and Bolivia on the west.

The Major Administrative Divisions of Paraguay number 17: the 16 Departments and the one Capital District.

Major Administrative Div.	Capital of Major Adm. Div.
1. Alto Paraná Department	Tacurupucú
2. Amambay Department	Pedro Juan Cabellero
3. Boquerón Department	Moriscal Estigarriba
4. Caaguazú Department	Coronel Oviedo
5. Caazapá Department	Caazapá
6. Central Department	Asunción
7. Concepción Department	Concepción
8. Guairá Department	Villarrica
9. Itapua Department	Encarnación
10. Las Cordilleras Department	Caapucú
11. Misiones Department	San Juan Bautista
12. Ñeembucu Department	Pilar
13. Olímpo Department	Fuerte Olímpo
14. Paraguarí Department	Paraguarí
15. Presidente Hayes Department	Villa Hayes
16. San Pedro Department	San Pedro
17. Capital District	Asunción

Peru (popular name)

The Republic of Peru (official name)

'Republica del Peru" (native name)

Lima (national capital)

Peru is located in Northwestern South America. It is
bounded by Ecuador on the north; by Colombia and Brazil
on the northeast and east; by Bolivia on the southeast; by
Chile on the south; and by the Pacific Ocean on the west.

The Major Administrative Divisions of Peru are the 24 Departments.

The minor administrative divisions of Peru are the 141 provinces and the 1321 districts.

	Departments	Capitals of Departments
1.	Amazones	Chachapoys
2.	Ancash	Huaras
3.	Apurímac	Abancay
4.	Arequipa	Arequipa
5.	Ayacucho	Ayacucho
6.	Cajamarca	Cajamarca
7.	Callao	Callao
8.	Cusco	Cusco
9.	Huarcavelica	Huarcavelica
10.	Huanuco	Huanuco
11.	Ica	Ica
12.	Junín	Huancayo
13.	La Libertad	Trujillo
14.	Lambayeque	Chiclayo
15.	Lima	Lima
16.	Lareto	Iquitos
17.	Madre de Dios	Puerto Maldonado
18.	Moquegua	Moquegua
19.	Pasco	Cerro de Pasco
20.	Piura	Piura
21.	Puno	Puno
22.	San Martín	Moyobamba
23.	Tacna	Tacna
24.	Tumbes	Tumbes

Philippines (popular name)

The Republic of the Philippines (official name)

"Republika ñg Pilipinas" (native name)

Quezon City (national capital)

The Philippines is located in Southeast Asia, and it is an
island country in the southwest Pacific Ocean. It is
bounded by the Luzon Straights on the north; by the Phil-
ippine Sea on the east; by the Celebes Sea on the south;
by the Sulu Sea on the southwest; and by the South China
Sea on the west.

The Major Administrative Divisions are the 56 Provinces.

The minor administrative divisions are the 41 Chartered
Cities, the districts, municipalities, and "barrios."

	Provinces	Provincial Capitals
1.	Batanes	Basco
2.	Cagayan	Tuguegarao
3.	Ilocos Norte	Lavag
4.	Ilocos Sur	Vigan
5.	Abra	Bangued
6.	Mountain	Bontoc
7.	Isabela	Ilagan
8.	Nueva Vizcaya	Bayombong
9.	La Union	San Fernando
10.	Pangasinam	Lingayen
11.	Nueva Ecija	Cabanatuan
12.	Tarlac	Tarlac
13.	Zambales	Iba
14.	Pampanga	San Fernando
15.	Bulacan	Malolas
16.	Quezon	Quezon
17.	Rizal	Pasig
18.	Bataan	Balanga
19.	Cavite	Cavite
20.	Laguna	Santa Cruz
21.	Batangas	Batangas
22.	Camarines Norte	Daet
23.	Camarines Sur	Naga
24.	Catanduanes	Virac
25.	Albany	Legaspi
26.	Marinduque	Boac
27.	Mindoro Oriental	Calapan

28.	Mindoro Occidental	Mindoro
29.	Romblon	Romblon
30.	Sorsogon	Sorsogon
31.	Masbate	Masbate
32.	Samar	Catbalogan
33.	Leyte	Tacloban
34.	Southern Leyte	Massin
35.	Aklan	Kalibo
36.	Roxas	Roxas
37.	Iloilo	Iloilo
38.	Antique	San Jose de Buenavista
39.	Palawan	Puerto Princessa
40.	Negros Occidental	Bacolod
41.	Negros Oriental	Dumaguete
42.	Cebu	Cebu
43.	Bohol	Tagbilaran
44.	Surigao del Norte	Surigao
45.	Surigao del Sur	Tandag
46.	Agusan	Butuan
47.	Misamis Oriental	Cagayan de Oro
48.	Misamis Occidental	Ozamiz
49.	Bukidon	Malaybalay
50.	Cotabato	Cotabato
51.	Lanao del Norte	Iligan
52.	Lanao del Sur	Dansalan
53.	Zamboanga del Norte	Dipolog
54.	Zamboanga del Sur	Zamboanga
55.	Sulu	Jolo
56.	Davao	Davao

Poland (popular name)

The Polish Republic (official name)

"Polska Rzeczpospolita Ludowa" (native name)

Warsaw (national capital)

Poland is located in Central Europe. It is bounded by the Baltic Sea on the north; by the U.S.S.R. on the east; by Czechoslovakia on the south; and by East Germany on the west.

The Major Administrative Divisions of Poland number 22: the 17 Provinces or "voivodships" and the 5 County Boroughs.

The minor administrative divisions of Poland are the 397

Poland (continued)

counties or "powait," the 8122 rural communes or "gromada," the 742 cities and towns, and the 136 settlements.

Major Administrative Div.	Capitals of Major Adm. Div.
1. Bialystock Province	Bialystok
2. Bydgoszcz Province	Bydgoszcz
3. Gdánsk Province	Gdánsk
4. Kielce Province	Kielce
5. Koszalin Province	Koszalin
6. Kraków Province	Kraków
7. Lódź Province	Lódź
8. Zielona Góra Province	Zielona Góra
9. Lublin Province	Lublin
10. Olsztyn Province	Olsztyn
11. Opole Province	Opole
12. Poznán Province	Poznán
13. Rzeszów Province	Rzeszów
14. Katowice Province	Katowice
15. Szczecin Province	Szczecin
16. Warszawa Province	Warszawa
17. Wroclaw Province	Wroclow
18. Lodz County Borough	Lodz
19. Warszawa County Borough	Warszawa
20. Wroclaw County Borough	Wroclaw
21. Poznan County Borough	Poznan
22. Kraców County Borough	Kraców

Portugal (popular name)

The Republic of Portugal (official name)

"Republica Portuguesa" (native name)

Lisbon (national capital)

Portugal is located in Southern Europe, on the western side of the Iberian Peninsula. It is bounded by Spain on the north and east; and by the Atlantic Ocean on the south and west.

The Major Administrative Divisions of Portugal number 40: the 11 continental provinces or "províncias;" the 22 districts or "distritos;" and the 7 overseas provinces.

The minor administrative divisions of Portugal are the 303

communes or "concelhos;" the boroughs or "bairros;" and the close to 4000 parishes or "freguesias."

Major Administrative Div.	Capitals of Major Adm. Div.
1. Algarve Province	Faro
2. Alto Alentejo Province	Évora
3. Baixo Alentejo Province	Beja
4. Beira Baixa Province	Castelo Branco
5. Beira Litoral Province	Coimbra
6. Douro Litoral Province	Porto
7. Beira Alta Province	Viseu
8. Estramadura Province	Lisbon
9. Minho Province	Braga
10. Ribatejo Province	Santarém
11. Trás-os-Montes e Alto Douro Province	Vila Real
12. Aveiro District	Aveiro
13. Beja District	Beja
14. Braga District	Braga
15. Bragança District	Bragança
16. Castelo Branco District	Castelo Branco
17. Coimbra District	Çoimbra
18. Évora District	Évora
19. Faro District	Faro
20. Guarda District	Guarda
21. Leiria District	Leiria
22. Lisboa District	Lisboa
23. Portalegre District	Portalegre
24. Porto District	Porto
25. Santarém District	Santarém
26. Setúbal District	Setúbal
27. Viana do Castelo District	Viana do Castelo
28. Vila Real District	Vila Real
29. Viseu District	Viseu
30. Angra Do Heroismo District	Angra Do Heroismo
31. Funchal District	Funchal
32. Horta District	Horta
33. Ponta Delgada District	Ponta Delgada
34. Angola (Overseas) Province	Luanda
35. Portuguese Guinea (Overseas) Province	Bissau
36. Cape Verde Islands (Overseas) Province	Praia
37. Mozambique (Overseas) Province	Lourenço Marques
38. Macao (Overseas) Province	Macao
39. Portuguese Timor (Overseas) Province	Dili

Portugal (continued)

Major Administrative Div.	Capitals of Major Adm. Div.
40. São Tomé e Príncipe (Overseas) Province	São Tomé

Further notes on the administrative divisions of Overseas Provinces.

Angola has 14 districts, as follows:

Districts	District Capitals
1. Benguela	Benguela
2. Bié-Cuando Cubango	Silva Porto
3. Cabinda	Cabinda
4. Cuanza Norte	Salazar
5. Cuanza Sul	Novo Redondo
6. Huambo	Nova Lisboa
7. Huila	Sá da Bandeira
8. Luanda	Luanda
9. Lunda	Henrique de Carvalho
10. Malanje	Malanje
11. Moçâmedes	Moçâmedes
12. Moxico	Luso
13. Uige	Carmona
14. Zaire	São Salvador

Portuguese Guinea has 3 "concelhos" and 8 "circunscriçãos," as follows:

Concelho	Concelho Capitals
1. Bafatá	Bafatá
2. Bissau	Bissau
3. Bolama	Bolama

Circunscrição	Circunscrição Capitals
1. Bajagós	Bubaque
2. Cacheu	Teixeira Pinto
3. Catió	Catió
4. Farim	Farim
5. Falacunda	Falacunda
6. Gabu	Nova Lamengo
7. Mansõa	Mansõa
8. São Domingos	São Domingos

Cape Verde Islands has 12 "concelhos."

Mozambique has 9 districts, as follows:

Districts	District Capitals
1. Capo Delgado	Porto Amélia
2. Gaza	Vila de João Belo
3. Inhambane	Inhambane
4. Lourenço Marques	Lourenço Marques
5. Tete	Tete
6. Manica e Sofala	Beira
7. Moçambique	Nampula
8. Niassa	Vila Cabral
9. Zambézia	Quelimane

Macao has 2 "concelhos."

Portugues Timor has 8 "circunscriçãos."

São Tomé e Príncipe has 2 "concelhos."

Qatar (popular name)

The Emirate of Qatar (official name)

Doha (national capital)

Qatar is located in Southwestern Asia, on the Arabian Peninsula. It is bounded by the Persian Gulf on the west, north, and east; and by Saudi Arabia on the south.

According to information available, currently The Emirate of Qatar has no administrative subdivisions except the Municipality of Doha.

Rhodesia (popular name)

Salisbury (national capital)

Rhodesia is located in South-central Africa. It is bounded by Zambia on the north; by Mozambique on the east; by South Africa on the south; and by Bechuanaland and Angola on the west.

The Major Administrative Divisions of Rhodesia are the 6 Provinces.

The minor administrative divisions are the 52 native districts.

Rhodesia (continued)

Provinces	Provincial Capitals
1. Manicaland	Umtali
2. Midlands	Gwelo
3. Northern Mashonaland	Salisbury
4. Northern Matabeleland	
5. Southern Mashonaland	Fort Victoria
6. Victoria	
7. Southern Matabeleland	Bulawayo

Rumania (popular name)

The Rumanian People's Republic (official name)

"Republica Populara Romåna" (native name)

Bucharest (national capital)

Rumania is located in East-central Europe. It is bounded by the U.S.S.R. on the north; by the U.S.S.R. and the Black Sea on the east; by Bulgaria on the south; and by Yugoslavia and Hungary on the west.

The Major Administrative Divisions of Rumania number 18: the 16 Administrative Regions or "regiunes;" the City of Constanta and the City of Bucharest.

The minor administrative divisions of Rumania are the 154 districts or "raions," the 181 towns, the 4290 rural communes, and the 15,133 villages.

Major Administrative Div.	Capitals of Major Adm. Div.
1. Arges Region	Pitesti
2. Bacau Region	Bacau
3. Banat Region	Timisoara
4. Brasov Region	Brasov
5. Bucharest Region	Bucharest
6. Cluj Region	Cluj
7. Crisana Region	Oradea
8. Dobrogea Region	Constanta
9. Galatzi Region	Galatzi
10. Hunedoara Region	Deva
11. Jassy Region	Jassy
12. Maramures Region	Baia-Mare
13. Mures Autonoma Maghiara Region	Tirgu Mures

14.	Oltenia Region	Craiova
15.	Ploiesti Region	Ploiesti
16.	Suceava Region	Suceava
17.	The City of Constanta	
18.	The City of Bucharest	

Rwanda (popular name)

The Republic of Rwanda (official name)

"La République Rwandaise" (native name)

Kigali (national capital)

Rwanda is located in East-central Africa. It is bounded by Uganda on the north; by Tanzania on the east; by Burundi on the south; and by Congo (Léopoldville) on the west.

The Major Administrative Divisions of Rwanda are the 10 Prefectures.

The minor administrative divisions of Rwanda are the 141 communes.

	Prefectures	Capitals of Prefectures
1.	Gikongoro	Gikongoro
2.	Cyangugu	Cyangugu
3.	Kibungo	Kibungo
4.	Kigali	Kigali
5.	Gitarama	Gitarama
6.	Kibuye	Kibuye
7.	Gisenyi	Gisenyi
8.	Ruhengeri	Ruhengeri
9.	Byumba	Byumba
10.	Butare	Butare

San Marino (popular name)

The Republic of San Marino (official name)

"Republica di San Marino" (native name)

San Marino (national capital)

San Marino is a tiny republic located in Southern Europe; situated on the slope of Mount Titano in the Apennines Mountains near Rimini, in the heart of Italy.

San Marino (continued)

The Major Administrative Divisions of San Marino are the
10 Circumscriptions.

Circumscriptions	Capitals of Circumscriptions
1. Aquaviva	Aquaviva
2. Borgo	Borgo
3. Chiesanuova	Chiesanuova
4. Domagnano	Domagnano
5. Faetano	Faetano
6. Fiorentino	Fiorentino
7. La Pleve	La Pleve
8. Montegiardino	Montegiardino
9. Sarravalle	Sarravalle
10. San Giovanni	San Giovanni

Saudi Arabia (popular name)

The Kingdom of Saudi Arabia. (official name)

"Al-Mamlaka Al-'Arabiya As-Sa'udiya" (native name)

Riyadh (national capital)

Saudi Arabia is located in southwestern Asia and occupies
four-fifths of the Arabian Peninsula. It is bounded by the
Persian Gulf, Qatar, and The Trucial States on the east;
by Muscat And Oman and Aden on the South and southeast;
by Yemen on the southwest; by the Red Sea and the Gulf
of Agaba on the west; and by Jordan, Iraq and Kuwait
on the north.

The Major Administrative Divisions of Saudi Arabia number
6: the 4 Provinces and the 2 Neutral Zones.

The minor administrative divisions are called districts.

Major Administrative Div.	Capitals of Major Adm. Div.
1. Hejaz Province	Mecca
2. Nejd Province	Riyadh
3. Asir Province	Abha
4. Eastern Province	Dammam
5. The Saudi-Arabian-Kuwaiti Neutral Zone	
6. The Saudi-Arabian-Iraqi Neutral Zone	

Senegal (popular name)

The Republic of Senegal (official name)

"République de Sénégal" (native name)

Dakar (national capital)

Senegal is located in Western Africa. It is bounded by the
Atlantic Ocean on the west; by Mauritania on the north;
by Mali on the east; and by Guinea, Portuguese Guinea,
and Gambia on the south.

The Major Administrative Divisions of Senegal are the 7
"Régions."

The minor administrative divisions are the 28 "cercles" and
90 "arrondissements."

"Régions"	Capitals of "Régions"
1. Cassamance	Ziguinchor
2. Valeé du Fleuve	St-Louis
3. Thiès	Thiès
4. Diourbel	Diourbel
5. Sine-Saloum	Kaolack
6. Sénégal Oriental	Tambacounda
7. Cap-Vert	Dakar

Sierra Leone (popular name)

The Government of Sierra Leone (official name)

Freetown (national capital)

Sierra Leone is located in Western Africa. It is bounded by
Guinea on the north; by Guinea and Liberia on the east;
and by the Atlantic Ocean on the south and west.

The Major Administrative Divisions of Sierra Leone number
16: the 4 Provinces and the 12 Districts.

The minor administrative divisions of Sierra Leone are the
urban and rural district councils.

Major Administrative Div.	Capitals of Major Adm. Div.
1. Eastern Province	Kenema
2. Northern Province	Makeni
3. Southern Province	Bo

Sierra Leone (continued)

Major Administrative Div.	Capitals of Major Adm. Div.
4. Western Province	Freetown
5. Koinadugu District	Kabala
6. Tonkolili District	Magburaka
7. Bombali District	Makani
8. Port Loko District	Port Loco
9. Kambia District	Kambia
10. Bo District	Bo
11. Moyamba District	Moyamba
12. Bonthe District	Bonthe
13. Pujehun District	Pujehun
14. Kono District	Sefadu
15. Kenema District	Kenema
16. Kailahun District	Kailahun

Sikkim (popular name)

The Kingdom of Sikkim (official name)

Gangtok (national capital)

Sikkim is a protectorate of India in Southern Asia.   It is
    bounded by Tibet on the north; by Bhutan on the east; by
    India on the south; and by Nepal on the west.

Sikkim's Administrative Divisions are the 3 Provinces
    called "Tahsils."

"Tahsils"
1. Eastern Tahsil (Lepchas)
2. Northern Tahsil (Bhutias)
3. Western Tahsil (Nepalese)

Singapore (popular name)

The State of Singapore (official name)

"Majúlah Singapura" (native name)

Singapore City (national capital)

Singapore is located in Southeast Asia, at the southern tip
    of the Malay Peninsula.   It is bounded by the Singapore
    Straights on the south; by the Straights of Jahore on the
    north; by the Straights of Malacca on the west; and by
    the South China Sea on the east.

Singapore's Administrative Divisions are its 6 Districts.

Districts
1. Singapore City
2. Bukit Panjang
3. Jurong
4. Katong
5. Serangoon
6. Southern Islands

Somalia (popular name)

The Somali Republic (official name)

Mogadishu (national capital)

Somalia is located in Eastern Africa. It is bounded by the
Gulf of Aden on the north; by the Indian Ocean on the
east and south; by Kenya and Ethiopia on the west; and
by French Somaliland on the northwest.

The Major Administrative Divisions of Somalia are the 8 Administrative Regions.

The minor administrative divisions of Somalia are the 30
districts.

Regions	Regional Capitals
1. Mijertein	Bender Kassim
2. Hiran	Belet Wein
3. Mudug	Galkayo
4. Benadir	Mogadishu
5. Alto Juba	Baidoa
6. Basso Juba	Kismayo
7. Hargeisa	Hargeisa
8. Burao	Burao

South Africa (popular name)

The Republic of South Africa (official name)

"Republiek Van Suid-Africa" (native name)

Pretoria (national capital)

South Africa is located in Southern Africa. It is bounded by
the Atlantic Ocean on the west; by South-West Africa on

South Africa (continued)

the northwest; by Bechuanaland and Rhodesia on the north; by the Indian Ocean on the east; and by Mozambique and Swaziland on the northeast.

The Major Administrative Divisions of South Africa number 5: the 4 Provinces and the one "Mandate."

The minor administrative divisions are the following types of "authorities:" Bantu (one of which is The Transkei with its capital at Umtata); Territorial; Regional; and Magisterial.

Major Administrative Div.	Capitals of Major Adm. Div.
1. The Cape Province	Capetown
2. Natal Province	Pietermaritzburg
3. Orange Free State Province	Bloemfontein
4. Transvaal Province	Pretoria
5. The South-West Africa Mandate	Windhoek

South Arabia, Federation of (popular name)

The Federation of South Arabia (official name)

"Ittihad al Janub al 'Arabi" (native name)

Al-Ittihad (national capital)

South Arabia is located in Southwestern Asia, and occupies a peninsula on the Arabian coast at the southern end of the Red Sea. It is bounded by the Gulf of Aden on the east and south; by Yemen on the west; and by Saudi Arabia on the north.

The Major Administrative Divisions of South Arabia are the 14 associated states having representation in the Federal Government.

States	State Capitals
1. The Aden State	Aden
2. The State of Dathina	Mudiyah
3. The Sultanate of Audhali	Zarah
4. The Sultanate of Lower Yafa	Ja'ar
5. The Sultanate of Lower Aulaqi	Ahwar
6. The Sultanate of Lahej	Hawtah
7. The Wahidi Sultanate of Balhaf	'Azzan

8.	The Haushabi Sultanate	Musaymir
9.	The Emirate of Baihan	al-Qisab
10.	The Emirate of Dhala	al-Dali'
11.	The Sheikdom of Upper Aulaqi	Ansab
12.	The Sheikdom of Sha'ib	Awabil
13.	The Sultanate of Fadhli	Al-Zanjabar
14.	The Sheikdom of 'Aqrabi	Bi'r Ahmad

South Arabia, Protectorate of (popular name)

The South Arabian Protectorate (official name)

Aden (capital) Note: Aden is located in the South Arabian Federation.

The South Arabian Protectorate is located in southwestern Asia, and occupies a peninsula on the Arabian coast at the southern end of the Red Sea. It is bounded by the Gulf of Aden on the east and south; by Yemen on the west; and by Saudi Arabia on the north.

The Major Administrative Divisions of The South Arabian Protectorate are the 14 Arabian states of this area not associated with The South Arabian Federation.

	States	State Capitals
1.	The Wahidi Sultanate of Bir'Ali	Bir 'Ali
2.	The Kathiri Sultanate of Sai'un	Sai'un
3.	The Mahra Sultanate of Qishn and Socotra	Tamrida, Socotra I.
4.	The Sheikdom of Hawrah	Al-Hawrah
5.	The Sheikdom of 'Irqah	Al-'Irqah
6.	The Qa'ayti Sultanate of Shihr And Mukalla	Al-Mukalla
7.	The Sheikdom of 'Alawi	Al-Qash'ah
8.	The Sheikdom of Qataybi	Al-Thumayr
9.	The Sheikdom of Upper Yafa	Mahjaba
10.	The Sheikdom of Bu'si	Al-Hajar
11.	The Sheikdom of Dhubi	Dhi Sura
12.	The Sheikdom of Hadhrami	Al-Shibr
13.	The Sheikdom of Maflahi	Khalla
14.	The Sheikdom of Mausatta	Al-Qudma

Spain (popular name)

The Spanish State (official name)

"Estado Español" (native name)

Spain (continued)

Madrid (national capital)

Spain is located in Southwestern Europe. It is bounded by
   Portugal and the Atlantic Ocean on the west; by France
   and The Bay of Biscay on the north; and by the Atlantic
   Ocean and the Mediterranean Sea on the east and west.

The Major Administrative Divisions of Spain number 55:
   the 50 metropolitan provinces, the 4 African provinces,
   and the "Plazas de Soberania" (of Northern Morocco).

The minor administrative divisions of Spain are the 9,000
   townships or "municipios."

Major Administrative Div.	Capitals of Major Adm. Div.
1. Almería Province	Almería
2. Cádiz Province	Cádiz
3. Córdoba Province	Córdoba
4. Granada Province	Granada
5. Huelva Province	Huelva
6. Jaén Province	Jaén
7. Málaga Province	Málaga
8. Sevilla Province	Sevilla
9. Huesca Province	Huesca
10. Teruel Province	Teruel
11. Zaragossa Province	Zaragossa
12. Oviedo Province	Oviedo
13. Ciudad Real Province	Ciudad Real
14. Cuena Province	Cuena
15. Guadalajara Province	Guadaljara
16. Madrid Province	Madrid
17. Toledo Province	Toledo
18. Avila Province	Avila
19. Burgos Province	Burgos
20. Logroño Province	Logroño
21. Palencia Province	Palencia
22. Santander Province	Santander
23. Segovia Province	Segovia
24. Soria Province	Soria
25. Valladolid Province	Valladolid
26. Barcelona Province	Barcelona
27. Gerona Province	Gerona
28. Lérida Province	Lérida
29. Tarragona Province	Tarragona
30. Badajoz Province	Badajoz

31. Cáceres Province	Cáceres
32. La Coruña Province	La Coruña
33. Lugo Province	Lugo
34. Orense Province	Orense
35. Pontevedra Province	Pontevedra
36. León Province	León
37. Salamanca Province	Salamanca
38. Zamora Province	Zamora
39. Albacete Province	Albacete
40. Murcia Province	Murcia
41. Alicante Province	Alicante
42. Castellón Province	Castellón
43. Valencia Province	Valencia
44. Alava Province	Vitorio
45. Guipúzcoa Province	San Sebastian
46. Navarra Province	Pamplona
47. Vizcaya Province	Bilboa
48. Baleares Province	Palma de Mallorca
49. Las Palmas Province	Las Palmas
50. Santa Cruz de Tenerife Province	Santa Cruz de Tenerife
51. Spanish Sahara (Sahara Espanõl) Province	El Aaiúm
52. Río Muni (African) Province	Bata
53. Ifni (African) Province	Sidi Ifni
54. Fernando Po (African) Province	Santa Isabel
55. "Las Plazas de Soberanía (special territory)	

Further notes on non-metropolitan Spain:

Spanish Sahara is divided administratively into 4 territories or districts.

Río Muni is divided administratively into 11 "municipios." It is located in the Gulf of Guinea.

Ifni is divided administratively into 3 districts.

"Las Plazas de Soberanía" consist of:
1. Ceuta (City)
2. Melilla (City)
3. Islas Chafarinas
4. Peñon de Alhucemas
5. Peñon de Vélez de la Gomera
These are small bits of Spanish territory in Northern Morocco.

117

Spain (continued)

Fernando Po has 4 regional districts. Its location is in the Gulf of Guinea.

Sudan (popular name)

The Republic of Sudan (official name)

"Jamhuryat El-Sudan" (native name)

Khartoum (national capital)

Sudan is located in Northeastern Africa. It is bounded by Libya and The United Arab Republic on the north; by the Red Sea and Ethiopia on the east; by Uganada, Kenya, and Congo (Léopoldville) on the south; and by Chad and the Central African Republic on the west.

The Major Administrative Divisions of Sudan are the 9 Provinces or "mudiriyahs."

The minor administrative divisions are the 85 rural and municipal councils.

Provinces	Provincial Capitals
1. Bahr el Ghazel	Wau
2. Kordofan	Al-'Ubayd
3. Khartoum	Khartoum
4. An Nil al Azraq (Blue Nile)	Wad Madani
5. Ash Shamaliyah (Northern)	Al-Damar
6. Kessala	Kessala
7. Darfur	Al-Fashur
8. A'ali an Nil (Upper Nile)	Malakal
9. Al Istiwa'iyah (Equatoria)	Juba

Sweden (popular name)

The Kingdom of Sweden (official name)

"Konungariket Sverige" (native name)

Stockholm (national capital)

Sweden is located in Northwestern Europe. It is bounded by Norway on the west and north; by Finland, the Gulf of Bothnia, and the Baltic Sea on the east; and by Denmark on the southwest.

The Major Administrative Divisions of Sweden number 25:
the 24 Counties or "län" and the one Capital City.

The minor administrative divisions are the districts or
"domsaga;" the rural communes or "landkommun;" and
the urban communes or the "stadkommun."

Major Administrative Div.	Capitals of Major Adm. Div.
1. Alvsborgs County	Vanersborg
2. Blekinge County	Karlskrona
3. Gävleborgs	Gavle
4. Göteborgs och Bohus County	Goteborg
5. Götlands County	Visby
6. Hallands County	Halmstad
7. Jämtlands County	Ostersund
8. Jönköpings County	Jönköpings
9. Kalmar County	Kalmar
10. Kopparbergs County	Falun
11. Kristianstads County	Kristianstads
12. Kronobergs County	Vaxjo
13. Malmöhus County	Malmo
14. Nörrbottens County	Lulea
15. Örebro	Orebro
16. Östergötlands County	Linkoping
17. Skaraborgs County	Mariestad
18. Södermanlands County	Nykoping
19. Stockholms Län County	Stockholm
20. Uppsala County	Uppsala
21. Värmlands County	Karlstad
22. Västerbottens County	Umea
23. Västernörrlands County	Harnosand
24. Västmanlands County	Vasteras
25. Stockholms Stad (City)	Stockholm

Switzerland (popular name)

The Swiss Confederation (official name)

"Suisse" (native name)

Berne (national capital)

Switzerland is located in Central Europe.   It is bounded by
France on the west; by West Germany on the north; by
Austria and Italy on the east; and by Italy on the south.

The Major Administrative Divisions are the 25 Cantons (or
Half-Cantons)

119

Switzerland (continued)

Cantons	Capitals of Cantons
1. Aargau	Aargau
2. Appenzell Ausser-Rhoden	Herisau
3. Appenzell Inner-Rhoden	Appenzell
4. Basel Land	Leistal
5. Basel Stadt	Basel
6. Berne	Berne
7. Fribourg	Fribourg
8. Geneva	Geneva
9. Glarus	Glarus
10. Grisons	Chur
11. Lucerne	Lucerne
12. Neuchâtel	Neuchâtel
13. St. Gall	St. Gall
14. Schaffhausen	Schaffhausen
15. Schwyz	Schwyz
16. Solothurn	Solothurn
17. Thurgau	Frauenfeld
18. Ticini	Bellinzonna
19. Nidwalden	Stans
20. Obwalden	Sarnen
21. Uri	Altdorf
22. Valais	Sion
23. Vaud	Lausanne
24. Zug	Zug
25. Zurich	Zurich

Syria (popular name)

The Syrian Arab Republic (official name)

"Souriya" (native name)

Damascus (national capital)

Syria is located in Southwestern Asia in the area known as
the Middle East. It is bounded by Turkey on the north;
by Iraq on the east; by Jordan and Israel on the south;
and by Lebanon and the Mediterranean Sea on the west.

The Major Administrative Divisions of Syria are the 12
Provinces or "mohafazats."

The minor administrative divisions of Syria are the counties
or "mantikas" and the subdivisions of "mantikas" called
"nahiyas."

Provinces	Provincial Capitals
1. Damascus City	Damascus
2. Damascus	Damascus
3. Hama	Hama
4. Homs	Homs
5. Dera'a	Dera'a
6. Aleppo	Aleppo
7. Lattakia	Lattakia
8. Deir-ez-Zor	Deir-ez-Zor
9. Al Jubal ad Druze	Soueida
10. Hassetché	Hassetché
11. Raqqa	Raqqa
12. Idlib	Idlib

Tanzania (popular name)

The United Republic of Tanzania (official name)

Dar-es Salaam (national capital)

Tanzania is located in Eastern Africa; formerly the two countries united as "Tanzania" were called Tanganyika and Zanzibar. It is bounded by Uganda and Kenya on the north; by the Indian Ocean on the east; by Mozambique, Malawi, and Zambia on the south; and by Congo (Léopold-ville) on the west.

The Major Administrative Divisions of Tanzania number 20: the 17 Administrative Regions of Tanganyika and the 3 Administrative Districts of Zanzibar.

The minor administrative divisions of Tanzania are the administrative "areas;" the town councils; district councils; and the municipal councils.

Major Administrative Div.	Capitals of Major Adm. Div.
1. Arusha Region	Arusha
2. Coast Region	Dar Es Salaam
3. Dodoma Region	Dodoma
4. Iringa Region	Iringa
5. Kigoma Region	Kigoma
6. Kilimanjaro Region	Moshi
7. Mara Region	Mara
8. Morogoro Region	Morogoro
9. Mtwara Region	Mtwara
10. Mwanza Region	Mwanza
11. Ruvuma Region	Songea
12. Shinyanga Region	Shinyanga

121

Tanzania (continued)

Major Administrative Div.	Capitals of Major Adm. Div.
13. Singida Region	Singida
14. Tabora Region	Tabora
15. Tanga Region	Tanga
16. West Lake Region	Bukoba
17. Mbeya Region	Mbeya
18. The Urban District of Zanzibar	
19. The Rural District of Zanzibar	
20. Pemba Administrative District	

Further note: Zanzibar has the minor administrative divisions called "mudiria" and shehia."

Thailand (popular name)

The Kingdom of Thailand (official name)

"Prades Thai" (native name)

Bangkok (national capital)

Thailand is located in Southeastern Asia. It is bounded by Burma on the northwest and west; by the Gulf of Siam and Malaysia on the south; by Cambodia on the southeast; and by Laos on the east and north.

The Major Administrative Divisions of Thailand are the 71 Provinces or "changwads."

The minor administrative divisions are the 489 districts or "amphurs;" the 21 sub-districts; and the 4,533 communes or "tambons."

Provinces	Provincial Capitals
1. Phranakhorn	Phranakhorn
2. Thonburi	Thonburi
3. Nonthaburi	Nonthaburi
4. Pathumthani	Pathumthani
5. Nakhornpathom	Nakhornpathom
6. Ratburi	Ratburi
7. Phetburi	Phetburi
8. Singhburi	Singhburi
9. Kanchanaburi	Kanchanaburi
10. Chonburi	Chonburi
11. Chanthaburi	Chanthaburi
12. Chai-nat	Chai-nat

13.	Prachuapkirikhan	Prachuapkirikhan
14.	Cha-choengsao	Cha-choengsao
15.	Samutsakhorn	Samutsakhorn
16.	Samutsongkhram	Samutsongkhram
17.	Samutprakan	Samutprakan
18.	Lopburi	Lopburi
19.	Suphanburi	Suphanburi
20.	Phranakhornsri-ayuthaya	Phranakhornsri-ayuthaya
21.	Angthong	Angthong
22.	Nakhornnayok	Nakhornnayok
23.	Trat	Trat
24.	Saraburi	Saraburi
25.	Prachinburi	Prachinburi
26.	Rayong	Rayong
27.	Kalasin	Kalasin
28.	Khon-kaen	Khon-kaen
29.	Chayaphum	Chayaphum
30.	Nakhornphanom	Nakhornphanom
31.	Nakhornratchsima	Nakhornratchsima
32.	Nongkhai	Nongkhai
33.	Buriram	Buriram
34.	Mahasarakham	Mahasarakham
35.	Roi-et	Roi-et
36.	Loei	Loei
37.	Srisaket	Srisaket
38.	Sakonnakhorn	Sakonnakhorn
39.	Surin	Surin
40.	Ubonratch-thani	Ubonratch-thani
41.	Udornthani	Udornthani
42.	Chumphorn	Chumphorn
43.	Ranong	Ranong
44.	Suratthani	Suratthani
45.	Phang-nga	Phang-nga
46.	Nakhornsrithamrat	Nakhornsrithamrat
47.	Phuket	Phuket
48.	Krabi	Krabi
49.	Phatalung	Phatalung
50.	Trang	Trang
51.	Satun	Satun
52.	Songkhla	Songkhla
53.	Pattani	Pattani
54.	Yala	Yala
55.	Nara-thiwat	Nara-thiwat
56.	Kamphaengphet	Kamphaengphet
57.	Chiengrai	Chiengrai
58.	Chiengmai	Chiengmai
59.	Tak	Tak

Thailand (continued)

Provinces	Provincial Capitals
60. Nakhornsawan	Nakhornsawan
61. Nan	Nan
62. Phichit	Phichit
63. Phitsnulok	Phitsnulok
64. Phetchbun	Phetchbun
65. Phrae	Phrae
66. Maehongson	Maehongson
67. Lampang	Lampang
68. Lamphun	Lamphun
69. Sukho-thai	Sukho-thai
70. Uttaradit	Uttaradit
71. Uthai-thani	Uthai-thani

Togo (popular name)

The Republic of Togo (official name)

"République Togolaise" (native name)

Lomé (national capital)

Togo is located in Western Africa. It is bounded by Upper Volta on the north; by Dahomey on the east; by the Atlantic Ocean on the south; and by Ghana on the west.

The Major Administrative Divisions of Togo number 17: the 10 Districts or "régions" and the 7 Independent Cities or "communes de plein exercice."

Major Administrative Div.	Capitals of Major Adm. Div.
1. Tsévié Région	Tsévié
2. Palimé Région	Palimé
3. Anécho Région	Anécho
4. Atakpamé Région	Atakpamé
5. Sokodé Région	Sokodé
6. Lama-Kara Région	Lama-Kara
7. Bassari Région	Bassari
8. Mango Région	Mango
9. Dapango Région	Dapango
10. Lomé Région	Lomé
11. Lomé Commune	Lomé
12. Anécho Commune	Anécho
13. Palimé Commune	Palimé
14. Bassari Commune	Bassari

15. Atakpamé Commune	Atakpamé
16. Sokodé Commune	Sokodé
17. Tsévié Commune	Tsévié

Tonga (popular name)

The Kingdom of Tonga (official name)

Nuku'alofa   (national capital)

Tonga is an archipelago kingdom located in the South-central Pacific, lying east of the Fiji Islands.

The Major Administrative Divisions of Tonga are the 3 Provinces.

Provinces	Provincial Capitals
1. Vava'u	Neiafu
2. Ha'apai	Pangai
3. Tongatapu	Nuku'alofa

Trinidad And Tobago (popular name)

The Independent State of Trinidad And Tobago (official name)

Port-of-Spain (national capital)

Trinidad And Tobago is located just north of Venezuela.   It is an island nation, the most southerly of The West Indies Islands.

The Major Administrative Divisions of Trinidad And Tobago number 12: the 9 Counties; the 2 Boroughs; and the one City Capital.

The minor administrative divisions are the 29 Trinidad wards and the 7 Tobago parishes.

Major Administrative Div.	Capitals of Major Adm. Div.
1. Caroni County	Chaguanas
2. Nariva County	Rio Claro
3. Mayaro County	Rio Claro
4. St. Andrew County	Sangre Grande
5. St. David County	Sangre Grande
6. St. George County	Tunapuna
7. St. Patrick County	Siparia
8. Victoria County	Princes Town
9. Tobago County	Scarborough

Trinidad And Tobago (continued)

Major Administrative Div.	Capitals of Major Adm. Div.
10. San Fernando Borough	San Fernando
11. Arima Borough	Arima
12. Port-of-Spain City	Port-of-Spain

Trucial States (popular name)

Trucial Oman (official name)

Dubai (chief center)

The Trucial States are a loose grouping of Arabian sheik-
doms in treaty arrangements with the United Kingdom.
They are located in Southwestern Asia on the Arabian
Peninsula. They are bounded by the Persian Gulf on the
north; by Muscat And Oman on the southeast; and by
Saudi Arabia on the south and west.

The Trucial States	Capitals of The Trucial States
1. State of Abu Dhabi	Abu Dhabi
2. State of Ajman	Ajman
3. State of Dubai	Dubai
4. State of Fujairah	Fujairah
5. State of Ras al Khaimah	Ras al Khaimah
6. State of Qaiwan	Qaiwan
7. State of Sharjah And Kalba	Sharjah

The Trucial States contain 18 districts:
1. 'Aqal
2. 'Aqalah
3. Al Bainumah
4. Batin
5. Al-Bitanah
6. Al-Dhafrah
7. Al-Dhahirah
8. Al-Jafurah
9. Al-Jau
10. Al-Khatam
11. Al-Kidan
12. Liwa
13. Al-Mijan
14. Al-Qufa
15. Ramlat al-Hamra
16. Rub 'al-Khali
17. Sabkhat Matti
18. Al-Taff

Tunisia (popular name)

The Republic of Tunisia (official name)

"République Tonisienne" (native name)

Tunis (national capital)

Tunisia is located in Northern Africa. It is bounded by the Mediterranean Sea on the north and east; by Libya on the southeast and south; and by Algeria on the west.

The Major Administrative Divisions of Tunisia are the 13 Regional Governorates or "gouvernats."

The minor administrative divisions are the 82 territorial delegations or "délegations" and the many "sheikhates."

Governorates	Capitals of Governorates
1. Tunis	Tunis
2. Beja	Beja
3. Bizerta	Bizerta
4. Cap Bon	Cap Bon
5. Gabes	Gabes
6. Gafsa	Gafsa
7. Kairouan	Kairouan
8. Kef	Kef
9. Medenine	Medenine
10. Sbeitla	Sbeitla
11. Sfax	Sfax
12. Souk-El-Arba	Souk-El-Arba
13. Sousse	Sousse

Turkey (popular name)

The Republic of Turkey (official name)

"Türkiye Cümhuriyetti" (native name)

Ankara (national capital)

Turkey is located in Eastern Europe and Western Asia. It is bounded by Bulgaria on the north; by Greece and the Aegean Sea on the west; by Iraq, Syria, and the Mediterranean Sea on the south; by Iran on the east; and by the U.S.S.R. on the northeast.

The Major Administrative Divisions of Turkey are the 67 Provinces or "iller."

Turkey (continued)

The minor administrative divisions of Turkey are the 493
districts or "ilceler," and the many communes or "bucak."

Provinces	Provincial Capitals
1. Afyon Karahisar	Karakose
2. Agri	Agri
3. Amasya	Amasya
4. Ankara	Ankara
5. Antalya	Antalya
6. Aydin	Aydin
7. Balikesir	Balikesir
8. Bilecik	Bilecik
9. Bingol	Capakcur
10. Bitlis	Bitlis
11. Bolu	Bolu
12. Burdur	Burdur
13. Bursa	Bursa
14. Canakkale	Canakkale
15. Cankiri	Cankiri
16. Corum	Corum
17. Denizli	Denizli
18. Diyarbakir	Diyarbakir
19. Edirne	Edirne
20. Elazig	Elazig
21. Erzincan	Erzincan
22. Erzurum	Erzurum
23. Eskisehir	Eskisehir
24. Gaziantep	Gaziantep
25. Giresun	Giresun
26. Gumashane	Gumashane
27. Hakkari	Hakkari
28. Hatay	Antakya
29. Icel	Mersin
30. Isparta	Isparta
31. Istanbul	Istanbul
32. Izmir	Izmir
33. Kars	Kars
34. Kastamonu	Kastamonu
35. Kayseri	Kayseri
36. Kirklareli	Kirklareli
37. Kirsehir	Kirsehir
38. Kocaeli	Izmit
39. Konya	Konya
40. Kutahya	Kutahya
41. Malatya	Malatya

42. Manisa	Manisa
43. Maras	Maras
44. Mardin	Mardin
45. Mugla	Mugla
46. Mus	Mus
47. Nigde	Nigde
48. Ordu	Ordu
49. Rize	Rize
50. Samsun	Samsun
51. Siirt	Siirt
52. Sinop	Sinop
53. Sivas	Sivas
54. Tekirdag	Tekirdag
55. Tokat	Tokat
56. Trabyon	Trabyon
57. Tunceli	Kalan
58. Urfa	Urfa
59. Van	Van
60. Yozgat	Yozgat
61. Zonguldak	Zonguldak
62. Adana	Adana
63. Adiyaman	Adiyaman
64. Artvin	Artvin
65. Nevsehir	Nevsehir
66. Sakarya	Sakarya
67. Usak	Usak

U. S. S. R. (popular name)

The Union of Soviet Socialist Republics (official name)

"Soyuz Sovetskikh Sotsialisticheskikh Respublik" (In Russian,
abbreviated as "C. C. C. P. ") (native name)

Moscow (national capital)

The U. S. S. R. is located both in Eastern Europe and Northern Asia. It is bounded by Finland, the Baltic Sea, Poland, Czechoslovakia, Hungary, and Rumania on the west;
by Rumania, the Black Sea, Turkey, Iran, Afghanistan,
China, Mongolia, and Korea on the south; by the Bering
Straights on the northeast; and by the Arctic Ocean on
the north.

The U. S. S. R. 's Major Administrative Divisions number 53:
the 15 Soviet Republics; the 20 Autonomous Republics;
the 8 Autonomous Regions or "oblasts;" and the 10 National Territories or "okrugs. "

U. S. S. R. (continued)

The minor administrative divisions of the U. S. S. R. include
their cities, villages, "rayons," "krays," and "oblasts"
(regions and districts).

Major Administrative Div.	Capitals of Major Adm. Div.
1. The Russian Soviet Federative Socialist Republic	Moscow
2. The Ukrainian Soviet Socialist Republic	Kiev
3. The Uzbek Soviet Socialist Republic	Tashkent
4. The Kazakh Soviet Socialist Republic	Alma-Ata
5. The Georgian Soviet Socialist Republic	Tbilisi
6. The Azerbaijan Soviet Socialist Republic	Baku
7. The Lithuanian Soviet Socialist Republic	Vilnius
8. The Moldavian Soviet Socialist Republic	Kishinev
9. The Latvian Soviet Socialist Republic	Riga
10. The Byelorussian Soviet Socialist Republic	Minsk
11. The Kirghiz Soviet Socialist Republic	Frunze
12. The Armenian Soviet Socialist Republic	Yerevan
13. The Tadzhik Soviet Socialist Republic	Dushanbe
14. The Turkmen Soviet Socialist Republic	Ashkhabad
15. The Estonian Soviet Socialist Republic	Tallinn
16. Bashkirian Autonomus Republic	Ufa
17. Buryat Autonomous Republic	Ulan-Ude
18. Daghestan Autonomous Republic	Mahachkala
19. Kabardinian-Balkar Autonomous Republic	Nalchik
20. Kalmyk Autonomous Republic	Elista
21. Karelian Autonomous Republic	Petrozavodsk
22. Komi Autonomous Republic	Syktyvkar
23. Mari Autonomous Republic	Voshkar-Ola
24. Mordovian Autonomous Republic	Sarask

25.	North Ossetian Autonomous Republic	Ordzhonikidze
26.	Tatar Autonomous Republic	Kazan
27.	Tuva Autonomous Republic	Kizyl
28.	Udmart Autonomous Republic	Izhevsk
29.	Checheno-Ingush Autonomous Republic	Grozny
30.	Chuvash Autonomous Republic	Cheboksary
31.	Yakut Autonomous Republic	Yakutsk
32.	Nakhichevan Autonomous Republic	Nakhichevan
33.	Abkhazian Autonomous Republic	Sukhumi
34.	Adjarian Autonomous Republic	Batumi
35.	Kara-Kalpak Autonomous Republic	Nukus
36.	Adygei Autonomous Region	Maikop
37.	Gorny Altai Autonomous Region	Gorno-Altaisk
38.	Jewish Autonomous Region	Birobidjan
39.	Karachai-Cherkess Autonomous Region	Cherkessk
40.	Khakass Autonomous Region	Abadan
41.	Nagorny Karabakh Autonomous Region	Stepanakert
42.	South Ossetian Autonomous Region	Tskhinvali
43.	Gorny Badakhshan Autonomous Region	Khorog
44.	Taymyr National Territory	Dudinka
45.	Evenki National Territory	Tura
46.	Nenets National Territory	Naryan-Mar
47.	Ust-Orda-Buryat National Territory	Ust-Ordynsky
48.	Koryak National Territory	Palana
49.	Chukchi National Territory	Anadyr
50.	Komi-Permyak National Territory	Kudymkar
51.	Khanty-Mansiysk National Territory	Khanty-Mansiysk
52.	Yamalo-Nenets National Territory	Salekhard
53.	Aga-Buryat National Territory	Aginskoye

Further notes on minor administrative divisions:
1. Byelorussia has 12 regions and 161 districts.
2. Russian S. F. S. R. has 6 territories, 49 regions, 5 autonomous regions within territories, and 10 national areas.
3. Uzbek has 9 regions and 148 districts.

4. Kazakh has 16 regions and 192 districts.
5. Georgia has 66 districts.
6. Azerbaijan has 68 districts.
7. Lithuania has 83 districts.
8. Moldavia has 40 districts.
9. Latvia has 45 districts.
10. Kirghiz has 5 regions and 44 districts.
11. Tadzhik has 47 districts.
12. Armenia has 33 districts.
13. Turkmen has 4 regions and 40 districts.
14. Estonia has 37 districts.
15. Ukraine has 26 regions.

Uganda (popular name)

The Republic of Uganda (official name)

Kampala (national capital)

Uganda is located in East-central Africa. It is bounded by
Sudan on the north; by Kenya on the east; by Tanzania
on the south; and by Congo (Léopoldville) on the west.

The Major Administrative divisions of Uganda number 23:
the 4 Regions and the 19 Administrative Districts.

Major Administrative Div.	Capitals of Major Adm. Div.
1. Eastern Region	Mbale
2. Western Region	Fort Portal
3. Buganda Region	Kampala
4. Northern Region	Gulu
5. Bugisu District	Mbale
6. Bukedi District	Mbale
7. Busoga District	Jinja
8. Territory of Mbale District	Mbale
9. Teso District	Soroti
10. Bunyoro District	Hoima
11. Toro District	Fort Portal
12. Ankole District	Mbarara
13. Kigezi District	Kabale
14. East Mengo District	Mengo
15. Masaka District	Masaka
16. Mubende District	Mubende
17. Karamoja District	Moroto
18. Lango District	Lira

19.	Acholi District	Gulu
20.	West Nile District	Arua
21.	West Mengo District	Mengo
22.	Seki District	Kapchorwa
23.	Madi District	Moyo

United Arab Republic (popular and official name)

"Al-Jumhuria Al-Arabia Al-Muttahida" (native name)

Cairo (national capital)

The United Arab Republic, formerly Egypt, is located in Northeastern Africa. It is bounded by Israel and the Red Sea on the east; by the Mediterranean Sea on the north; by Libya on the west; and by Sudan on the south.

The Major Administrative Divisions of the United Arab Republic are the 20 Governorates.

The minor administrative divisions of the United Arab Republic are the 216 municipal councils.

	Governorates	Capitals of Governorates
1.	Cairo	Cairo
2.	Alexandria	Alexandria
3.	Suez	Suez
4.	Port Said	Port Said
5.	Ismailia	Ismailia
6.	Damietta	Damietta
7.	Kafr el Sheikh	Kafr el Sheikh
8.	Giza	Giza
9.	Beni Suef	Beni Suef
10.	Faiyum	Faiyum
11.	Suhag	Suhag
12.	Qena	Qena
13.	Asyut	Asyut
14.	Minya	Minya
15.	Behera	Damanhur
16.	Gharbiya	Tanta
17.	Daqahiya	Mansura
18.	Sharqiya	Zagazig
19.	Menufiya	Shibin-el-Kom
20.	Qalyubiya	Benha

The United Kingdom of Great Britain and North Ireland (official name)

London (national capital)

The United Kingdom or The British Isles are located off the northwestern corner of continental Europe. It is bounded by the north Atlantic Ocean on the north and west; by the North Sea on the east; and by the English Channel on the south, which separates the United Kingdom from France.

The Major Administrative Divisions of the United Kingdom number 222 - they include:

a. England (capital-London) encompasses 48 Administrative Counties plus 79 County Boroughs

b. Wales (capital-Cardiff) encompasses 13 Administrative Counties plus 4 County Boroughs

c. Scotland (capital-Edinburgh) encompasses 33 Civil Counties plus 4 Counties-of-Cities

d. Northern Ireland (capital-Belfast) encompasses 6 Counties plus 2 County Boroughs

e. The 34 dependent or semi-dependent areas administered by the United Kingdom, called "Dependencies" below.

The Minor Administrative Divisions of the United Kingdom include municipal boroughs, urban districts, rural districts, and civil parishes.

Major Administrative Div.	Capitals of Major Adm. Div.
a. (England)	
1. Bedfordshire County	Bedford
2. Berkshire County	Reading
3. Buckinghamshire County	Aylesbury
4. Cambridgeshire County	Cambridge
5. Isle of Ely County	March
6. Cheshire County	Chester
7. Cornwall County	Truro
8. Cumberland County	Carlisle
9. Derbyshire County	Matlock
10. Devonshire County	Exeter

11.	Dorsetshire County	Dorchester
12.	Durham County	Durham
13.	Essex County	Chelmsford
14.	Gloucestershire County	Gloucester
15.	Hampshire County	Winchester
16.	Isle of Wight County	Newport
17.	Herefordshire County	Hereford
18.	Hertfordshire County	Hertford
19.	Huntingdonshire County	Huntingdon
20.	Kent County	Maidstone
21.	Lancashire County	Preston
22.	Leicestershire County	Leicester
23.	Lincolnshire County - The Parts of Holland	Boston
24.	Lincolnshire County - The Parts of Kesteven	Sleaford
25.	Lincolnshire County - The Parts of Lindsey	Lincoln
26.	London County	London
27.	Norfolk County	Norwich
28.	Northamptonshire County	Northampton
29.	Northumberland County	Newcastle-On-Tyne
30.	Nottinghamshire County	Nottingham
31.	Oxfordshire County	Oxford
32.	Soke of Peterborough County	Peterborough
33.	Rutlandshire County	Oakham
34.	Shropshire County	Shrewsbury
35.	Somersetshire County	Taunton
36.	Staffordshire County	Stafford
37.	East Suffolk County	Ipswich
38.	West Suffolk County	Bury St. Edmunds
39.	Surrey County	Kingston-On-Thames
40.	East Sussex County	Lewes
41.	West Sussex County	Chichester
42.	Warwickshire County	Warwick
43.	Westmorland County	Kendal
44.	Wiltshire County	Trowbridge
45.	Worcestershire County	Worcester
46.	Yorkshire County-East Riding	Beverly
47.	Yorkshire County-West Riding	Wakefield
48.	Yorkshire County-North Riding	Northallerton
49.	Barrow-In-Furness County Borough	
50.	Bath County Borough	
51.	Birkenhead County Borough	
52.	Birmingham County Borough	
53.	Blackburn County Borough	
54.	Blackpool County Borough	
55.	Bolton County Borough	

United Kingdom (continued)

Major Administrative Div.	Capitals of Major Adm. Div.
(a) (England)	

56. Bootle County Borough
57. Bournemouth County Borough
58. Bradford County Borough
59. Brighton County Borough
60. Bristol County Borough
61. Burnley County Borough
62. Burton-On-Trent County Borough
63. Bury County Borough
64. Canterbury County Borough
65. Carlisle County Borough
66. Chester County Borough
67. Coventry County Borough
68. Croydon County Borough
69. Darlington County Borough
70. Derby County Borough
71. Dewsbury County Borough
72. Doncaster County Borough
73. Dudley County Borough
74. Eastbourne County Borough
75. East Ham County Borough
76. Exeter County Borough
77. Gateshead County Borough
78. Gloucester County Borough
79. Grimsby County Borough
80. Halifax County Borough
81. Hastings County Borough
82. Huddersfield County Borough
83. Hull County Borough
84. Ipswich County Borough
85. Leeds County Borough
86. Leicester County Borough
87. Lincoln County Borough
88. Liverpool County Borough
89. Manchester County Borough
90. Middlesborough County Borough
91. Newcastle County Borough
92. Northampton County Borough
93. Norwich County Borough
94. Nottingham County Borough
95. Oldham County Borough
96. Oxford County Borough
97. Plymouth County Borough
98. Portsmouth County Borough
99. Preston County Borough

100. Reading County Borough
101. Rockdale County Borough
102. Rotherham County Borough
103. St. Helens County Borough
104. Salford County Borough
105. Sheffield County Borough
106. Smethwick County Borough
107. Southampton County Borough
108. Southend County Borough
109. Southport County Borough
110. South Shields County Borough
111. Stockport County Borough
112. Stoke-On-Trent County Borough
113. Sunderland County Borough
114. Tynemouth County Borough
115. Wakefield County Borough
116. Wallasey County Borough
117. Walsall County Borough
118. Warrington County Borough
119. West Bromwich County Borough
120. West Ham County Borough
121. West Hartlepool County Borough
122. Wigan County Borough
123. Wolverhampton County Borough
124. Worcester County Borough
125. Yarmouth County Borough
126. York County Borough
127. Barnsley County Borough

(b) (Wales)

128.	Anglesey County	Llangefni
129.	Flint County	Mold
130.	Denbigh County	Ruthbin
131.	Caernarvon County	Caernarvon
132.	Marioneth County	Dolgellau
133.	Montgomery County	Welshpool
134.	Radnor County	Llandrindod Wells
135.	Cardigan County	Aberystwyth
136.	Carmarthen County	Carmarthen
137.	Brecknock County	Brecon
138.	Pembroke County	Haverfordwest
139.	Glamorgan County	Cardiff
140.	Monmouth County	Newport
141.	Cardiff County Borough	
142.	Merthyr Tydfil County Borough	
143.	Newport County Borough	
144.	Swansea County Borough	

United Kingdom (continued)

Major Administrative Div.	Capitals of Major Adm. Div.
(c) (Scotland)	
145. Aberdeen County	Aberdeen
146. Angus County	Forfar
147. Argyll County	Lochgilphead
148. Ayr County	Argyll
149. Banff County	Ayr
150. Berwick County	Duns
151. Bute County	Rothesay
152. Caithness County	Wick
153. Clackmannan County	Alloa
154. Dumfries County	Dumfries
155. Dunbarton County	Dunbarton
156. East Lothian County	Haddington
157. Elgin County	Elgin
158. Fife County	Cupar
159. Inverness County	Inverness
160. Kincordine County	Stonehaven
161. Kinross County	Kinross
162. Kirkcudbright County	Kirkcudbright
163. Lanark County	Glasgow
164. Midlothian County	Edinburgh
165. Nairn County	Nairn
166. Orkney County	Kirkwall
167. Peebles County	Peebles
168. Perth County	Perth
169. Renfrew County	Paisley
170. Ross And Cromarty County	Dingwall
171. Roxburgh County	Newton St. Boswells
172. Selkirk County	Selkirk
173. Stirling County	Stirling
174. Sutherland County	Golspie
175. West Lothian County	Linlithgow
176. Wigtown County	Stranraer
177. Zetland County	Lerwick
178. Edinburgh County-of-City	
179. Glasgow County-of-City	
180. Aberdeen County-of-City	
181. Dundee County-of-City	
(d) (Northern Ireland)	
182. Antrin County	Belfast
183. Armagh County	Armagh
184. Down County	Downpatrick
185. Fermanagh County	Ennickillen
186. Londonerry County	Londerry

187. Tyrone County	Omagh
188. Belfast County Borough	
189. Londonerry County Borough	

(e) (Dependencies)

190. Turks And Caicos Islands	Grand Turk
191. Mauritius	Port Louis
192. New Hebrides	Port-Vila
193. Pitcairn	Adamstown
194. St. Helena	Jamestown
195. Seychelles	Victoria
196. Swaziland	Mbabane
197. Antigua	St. Johns
198. Barbados	Bridgetown
199. Montserrat	Plymouth
200. St. Kitts-Nevis-Anguilla	Basseterre
201. Dominica	Roseau
202. Grenada	St. George's
203. St. Lucia	Castries
204. St. Vincent	Kingstown
205. British Virgin Islands	Roadtown
206. British Antarctic Territories	Admiralty Bay
207. Cayman Islands	Georgetown, Grand Cayman
208. Bahama Islands	Nassau
209. Basutoland	Maseru
210. Bechuanaland	Gaberones
211. Bermuda	Hamilton
212. British Guiana*	Georgetown
213. British Honduras	Belize
214. Canton And Enderbury Is.	Canton Island
215. Falkland Is.	Stanley
216. Gibraltar	Gibraltar
217. Gilbert And Ellice Is.	Bairiki, Tarawa Is.
218. Guernsey	St. Peter Port
219. Isle of Man	Douglas
220. Jersey	St. Helier
221. Hong Kong	Hong Kong
222. Fiji Islands	Suva
223. British Solomon Is.	Honiara

*To be the new independent nation called "Guyana."

United Kingdom's Dependencies are sub-divided for purposes of administration as follows:

(a) The Isle of Man is divided into 6 Sheadings:
1. Rushen
2. Middle
3. Ayre

United Kingdom (continued)

<u>Isle of Man Sheadings</u>
    4. Garff
    5. Glenfaba
    6. Michael

(b) Bechuanaland is divided into 11 Districts:

Districts	Capitals of Districts
1. Ngamiland	Maun
2. Ngwato	Serowe
3. Gaberones	Gaberones
4. Francistown	Francistown
5. Kgatleng	Mochudi
6. Kweneng	Molepolole
7. Ngwaketse	Kanye
8. Lobatsi	Lobatsi
9. Kgalagadi	Tshabong
10. Ghanzi	Ghanzi
11. Kasane	Kasane

(c) The Colony of British Guiana is divied into 3 counties:
    1. Berbice
    2. Demerara
    3. Essequibo

British Honduras is divided into 6 districts:

1. Cayo	El Cayo
2. Corozal	Corozal
3. Stann Creek	Stann Creek
5. Toledo	Punta Gorda
6. Belize	Belize

(d) Gilbert and Ellice Islands Colony is divided into 5 districts:

1. Ellice Islands	Funafuti Island
2. Gilbert Islands	Bairiki, Tarawa Is.
3. Phoenix Islands	Canton Island
4. Northern Lini Islands	Fanning Island
5. Ocean Island	Ocean Island

(e) The British High Commissioner Territory of Swaziland is divided into 6 districts:

    1. Mbabane
    2. Bremersdorp
    3. Hlatikulu

4. Stegi
5. Pigg's Peak
6. Mankaiana

(f) Basutoland is divided into 9 districts:

1. Maseru
2. Mokhotlong
3. Qacha's Nek
4. Quthing
5. Mohale's Hoek
6. Mafeteng
7. Teyateyaneng
8. Leribe
9. Butha-Buthe

(g) The Colony of the Bahamas is divided into 19 districts:

1. Abaco
2. Andros Island
3. Berry Islands
4. Bimini Islands
5. Cat Island
6. Cay Lobos
7. Eleuthera
8. Exuma
9. Grand Bahama
10. Harbour Island
11. Inagua
12. Long Cay
13. Long Island
14. Mayaguana
15. New Providence
16. Ragged Island And Cays
17. Rum Cay
18. San Salvador
19. Spanish Wells

(h) The Colony of Barbados is divided into 11 Parishes:

1. Christ Church
2. St. Andrew
3. St. George
4. St. James
5. St. John
6. St. Joseph
7. St. Lucy
8. St. Michael

141

United Kingdom (continued)

(h) Colony of Barbados parishes (cont.)
   9. St. Peter
   10. St. Phillip
   11. St. Thomas

United States (popular name)

The United States of America (official name)

Washington, D. C. (national capital)

The United States is located in North America. It is bounded by Canada and The Great Lakes (in Alaska by the Arctic Ocean) on the north; by the Pacific Ocean on the west; by the Atlantic Ocean on the east; and by Mexico and the Gulf of Mexico on the south.

The Major Administrative Divisions of the United States number 58. They include: (a) the 50 States of the Union; (b) the 1 federal capital district; (c) the self-governing Commonwealth of Puerto Rico, and (d) the other 6 major dependencies.

The minor administrative divisions of the United States include over three thousand counties, a vast number of boroughs, organized boroughs, unorganized boroughs, towns, townships, independent cities, parishes, plantations, government reservations, villages, etc. (Also, at the end of this country's listing, the names of the U.S.A.'s 31 minor possessions will be found.)

Major Administrative Div.	Capitals of Major Adm. Div.
(a) States:	
1. Alabama	Montgomery
2. Alaska	Juneau
3. Arizona	Phoenix
4. Arkansas	Little Rock
5. California	Sacramento
6. Colorado	Denver
7. Connecticut	Hartford
8. Delaware	Dover
9. Florida	Tallahassee
10. Georgia	Atlanta
11. Hawaii	Honolulu
12. Idaho	Boise
13. Illinois	Springfield

14.	Indiana	Indianapolis
15.	Iowa	Des Moines
16.	Kansas	Topeka
17.	Kentucky	Frankfort
18.	Louisiana	Baton Rouge
19.	Maine	Augusta
20.	Maryland	Annapolis
21.	Massachusetts	Boston
22.	Michigan	Lansing
23.	Minnesota	St. Paul
24.	Mississippi	Jackson
25.	Missouri	Jefferson City
26.	Montana	Helena
27.	Nebraska	Lincoln
28.	Nevada	Carson City
29.	New Hampshire	Concord
30.	New Jersey	Trenton
31.	New Mexico	Santa Fe
32.	New York	Albany
33.	North Carolina	Raleigh
34.	North Dakota	Bismarck
35.	Ohio	Columbus
36.	Oklahoma	Oklahoma City
37.	Oregon	Salem
38.	Pennsylvania	Harrisburg
39.	Rhode Island	Providence
40.	South Carolina	Columbia
41.	South Dakota	Pierre
42.	Tennessee	Nashville
43.	Texas	Austin
44.	Utah	Salt Lake City
45.	Vermont	Montpelier
46.	Virginia	Richmond
47.	Washington	Olympia
48.	West Virginia	Charleston
49.	Wisconsin	Madison
50.	Wyoming	Cheyenne

(b) Federal District
51.	The District of Columbia	Washington

(c) The 1 Commonwealth
52.	Puerto Rico	San Juan

(d) The Dependencies
53.	Panama Canal Zone	Balboa Heights
54.	Virgin Is. of the U.S.A.	Charlotte Amalie
55.	American Samoa	Pago Pago

143

United States (continued)

(d) Dependencies (cont.)
56. Guam   Agaña
57. Ryukyu Islands   Naha, Okinawa
58. The Trust Territory of the
      Pacific Islands   Chalan Kanoa, Saipan

The dependencies are divided for administration as follows:

(a) The Trust Territory of the Pacific Islands include 6
     districts.

Districts	Capitals of Districts
1. Saipan	Chalan Kanoa
2. Palau	Koror
3. Yap	Yap Town
4. Truk	Moen
5. Ponape	Colonia
6. Marshall Is.	Majuro

(b) The Panama Canal Zone has 2 districts:

1. Cristobal
2. Balboa

(c) The Virgin Islands of the U. S. A. has 2 municipalities:

1. St. Croix Municipality
2. St. Thomas and St. John Municipality

(d) Guam has 15 municipalities

1. Agaña
2. Agat
3. Asan
4. Barrigada
5. Dededo
6. Inarajan
7. Machanao
8. Merizo
9. Piti
10. Sinaiana
11. Sumay
12. Talofof
13. Umatac
14. Yigo
15. Yona

(e) American Samoa comprises 4 districts and 14 counties
   as follows:

   1. Eastern Tutuila District
   2. Western Tutuila District
   3. Manu'a District
   4. Swains Island District
   5. Ituau County
   6. Mauputasi County
   7. Saole County
   8. Sua County
   9. Vaifanua County
   10. Lealataua County
   11. Leasina County
   12. Tualauta County
   13. Tualatai County
   14. Faleasao County
   15. Fitiuta County
   16. Ofu County
   17. Olosega County
   18. Ta'u County

Some of the States contain minor administrative divisions
   other than Counties.   They are:
   (a) Maine, with
                           21 cities
                          416 towns
                           56 plantations
                          407 unorganized townships
                           21 villages

   (b) Massachusetts with   39 cities
                          312 towns

   (c) New Hampshire with   13 cities
                          221 towns

   (d) New Jersey with   334 cities and towns
                          233 townships

   (e) New York with   62 cities
                          932 towns
                          550 incorporated villages, and
                            7 Indian reservations

   (f) Pennsylvania with 1003 cities, towns and boroughs
                         1556 townships, and
                            1 Indian reservation

United States (continued)

(g) Vermont with

8	cities
238	towns, and
60	incorporated villages

(h) Connecticut with

169	towns
23	cities
12	boroughs

(i) Rhode Island with

| 8 | cities and |
| 31 | towns |

(j) Alaska has

| 54 | cities and the following |
| 9 | organized boroughs |

Boroughs	Capitals of Boroughs
1. Bristol Bay	Naknek
2. Gateway	Ketchikan
3. Greater Juneau	Juneau
4. Greater Sitka	Sitka
5. Kodiak Island	Kodiak
6. Greater Anchorage	Anchorage
7. Matanuska-Susitna	Palmer
8. North Star	Fairbanks
9. Kenai Peninsula	Soldotna

The Commonwealth of Puerto Rico includes the following 77 municipalities or "municipales:"

1. Bayamon
2. Boa Alta
3. Boa Baja
4. Corozal
5. Gurabo
6. Juncos
7. Yabucoa
8. Maunabo
9. Carolina
10. Loiza
11. Rio Grande
12. Luquillo
13. Dorado
14. Barceloneta
15. Hatillo
16. Camuy
17. Guayama
18. Cayey

19. Arroyo
20. Patillas
21. Humacao
22. San Lorenzo
23. Las Piedras
24. Cataño
25. Naranjito
26. Comerioq
27. Barranquitas
28. Orocovis
29. Aibonito
30. Fajardo
31. Naguabo
32. Ceiba
33. Caguas
34. Aguas Buenas
35. Cidra
36. Manati
37. Vega Alta
38. Vega Baja
39. Morovis
40. Ciales
41. Arecibo
42. Utuado
43. Trujillo Alto
44. San Juan
45. Ponce
46. Ponce I
47. Ponce II
48. Adjuntas
49. Jayuya
50. Santa Isabel
51. Salinas
52. Villalba
53. Juana Diaz
54. Coamo
55. Peñuelas
56. Guayanilla
57. Yauco
58. Guanica
59. Mayaguez
60. Maricao
61. Las Marias
62. Hormigueros
63. Cabo Rojo
64. San German
65. Sabana Grande
66. Lajas

United States (continued)

Municipalities of Puerto Rico (cont.)
    67. Añasco
    68. Rincon
    69. Moca
    70. San Sebastian
    71. Lares
    72. Aguadilla
    73. Aguada
    74. Isabela
    75. Quebradillas
    76. Vieques
    77. Colebra

The 31 minor possessions of the U. S. A. are:

    1. Wake Islands
    2. Midway Islands
    3. Johnston And Sand Islands
    4. Kingman Reef
    5. Howland, Baker, and Jarvis Islands
    6. Canton Island and Enderbury Island
    7. Corn Islands ("Islas del Maiz")
    8. Swan Islands ("Islas de Ciscne")
    9. Palmyra Island
    10. Navassa Island
    11. Sand Island
    12. Caroline Island
    13. Christmas Island
    14. Danger Island ("Pukapuka")
    15. Flint Island
    16. Funafuti Island
    17. Malden Island
    18. Manahiki Island
    19. Nukufetau Island
    20. Nukulailui Island
    21. Nurakita Island
    22. Penrhyn Island
    23. Rakahanga Island
    24. Starbuck Island
    25. Vostok Island
    26. Phoenix Islands (except Canton and Enderbury)
    27. Union or Tokelau Islands
    28. Quita Sueño Bank
    29. Roncador Cay
    30. Serrana Bank
    31. Bonin, Volcano, and Marcus Islands

Upper Volta (popular name)

The Republic of Upper Volta (official name)

"République de Haut-Volta" (native name)

Ouagadougou (national capital)

Upper Volta is located in Western Africa. It is bounded by
Mali on the west and north; by Niger on the east; and by
Ivory Coast, Togo, and Dahomey on the south.

The Major Administrative Divisions of Upper Volta are the
5 "Départements."

The minor administrative divisions of Upper Volta are the
38 cercles, the 18 subdivisions, and the cantons and administrative posts.

Départements	Capitals of Départements
1. Est	Fada-Ngourma
2. Centre	Ouagadougou
3. Sahel	Ouahigouya
4. Hauts-Bassins	Koudougou
5. Volta-Noire	Bobo-Dioulasso

Uruguay (popular name)

The Oriental Republic of Uruguay (official name)

"Republica Oriental del Uruguay" (native name)

Montevideo (national capital)

Uruguay is located in Southern South America. It is
bounded by Brazil on the north and east; by the South Atlantic Ocean and the River Plata on the south; and by Argentina on the west.

The Major Administrative Divisions of Uruguay are the 19
Departments.

Departments	Capitals of Departments
1. Artigas	Artigas
2. Canelones	Canelones
3. Cerro Largo	Melo
4. Coloma	Coloma
5. Durazno	Durazno

Uruguay (continued)

Departments	Capitals of Departments
6. Flores	Trinidad
7. Florida	Florida
8. La Valleja	Minas
9. Maldonado	Maldonado
10. Montevideo	Montevideo
11. Paysandú	Paysandú
12. Rió Negro	Fray Bentos
13. Rivera	Rivera
14. Rocha	Rocha
15. Salto	Salto
16. San José	San José
17. Soriano	Mercedes
18. Tacuarembró	Tacuarembró
19. Trienta y Tres	Trienta y Tres

Vatican City (popular name)

The State of Vatican City (official name)

"Stato Della Citta Del Vaticano" (native name)

Vatican City (national capital)

Vatican City is located in southern Europe. It is the smallest independent country in the world, and houses the government of the Roman Catholic Church. It is entirely surrounded by the Italian capital of Rome.

As for administration, the lay government is by the Pope as sovereign but actual day-to-day civic affairs are handled by The Pontifical Commission.

Venezuela (popular name)

The Republic of Venezuela (official name)

"Republica de Venezuela" (native name)

Caracas (national capital)

Venezuela is located in Northern South America. It is bounded by the Caribbean Sea on the north; by British Guiana on the east; by Brazil on the southeast; and by Colombia on the southwest and west.

The Major Administrative Divisions of Venezuela number 24:
the 20 States; the 2 Federal Territories; the one Federal Capital; and the one Federal Island Dependency.

The minor administrative divisions are the municipalities.

Major Administrative Div.	Capitals of Major Adm. Div.
1. Anzoategui State	Barcelona
2. Apure State	San Fernando
3. Aragua State	Maracay
4. Barinas State	Barinas
5. Bolivar State	Ciudad Bolívar
6. Carabobo State	Valencia
7. Cojedes State	San Carlos
8. Falcon State	Coro
9. Guarico State	San Juan de los Morros
10. Lara State	Barquisimeto
11. Mérida State	Mérida
12. Miranda State	Los Teques
13. Monagas State	Maturin
14. Nueva Esparta State	La Asuncion
15. Portuguesa State	Guanare
16. Sucre State	Cumaná
17. Tachira State	San Cristóbal
18. Trujillo State	Trujillo
19. Yaracuy State	San Felipe
20. Zulia State	Maracaibo
21. Delta Amacura Territory	Tucupita
22. Amazonas Territory	Puerto Ayacucho
23. Distrito Federal	Caracas
24. Las Dependancias Federales Por Islas	Los Roques Island

(Vietnam) North Vietnam (popular name)

The Democratic People's Republic of Viet-Nam (official name)

"Viet Nam Dan Chu Cong Hoa" (native name)

Hanoi (national capital)

North Vietnam is located in Southeast Asia. It is bounded
by China on the north; by the South China Sea on the east;
by South Vietnam on the south; and by Laos on the west.

The Major Administrative Divisions of North Vietnam number
33: the 28 Provinces or "tinh;" the 2 Autonomous Regions;

Vietnam (continued)

the 1 Special Zone; and the 2 Centrally-administered municipalities.

The minor administrative divisions of North Vietnam are the districts or "huyen" and the divisions known as "chai" and "phu."

Major Administrative Div.	Capitals of Major Adm. Div.
1. Lai Chau Province	Lai Chau
2. Nghia Los Province	Nghia Lo
3. Son La Province	Son La
4. Ha Giang Province	Ha Giang
5. Cao Bang Province	Cao Bang
6. Tuyen Quang Province	Tuyen Quang
7. Bac Can Province	Bac Can
8. Thai Nguyen Province	Thai Nguyen
9. Lang Son Province	Lang Son
10. Lao Cai Province	Lao Cai
11. Yen Bai Province	Yen Bai
12. Phu Tho Province	Phu Tho
13. Vinh Phuc Province	Vinh Yen
14. Ha Bac Province	Bac Ninh
15. Hoa Binh Province	Hoa Binh
16. Son Tay Province	Son Tay
17. Ha Dong Province	Ha Dong
18. Hung Yen Province	Hung Yen
19. Hai Duong Province	Hai Duong
20. Thanh Hoa Province	Thanh Hoa
21. Ninh Binh Province	Ninh Binh
22. Ha Nam Province	Phu Ly
23. Nam Dinh Province	Nam Dinh
24. Thai Binh Province	Thai Binh
25. Nghe An Province	Vinh
26. Ha Tinh Province	Ha Tinh
27. Quang Binh Province	Ron
28. Quang Ninh Province	Hon Gai
29. Vinh Linh Special Zone	
30. Hanoi Municipality	
31. Haiphong Municipality	
32. Viet-Bac Autonomous Region	
33. Tay-Bac Autonomous Region	

(Vietnam) South Vietnam (popular name)

The Republic of South Vietnam (official name)

"Viet-Nam Cong Hoa" (native name)

Saigon (capital city)

South Vietnam is located in Southeast Asia. It is bounded
by North Vietnam on the north; by the South China Sea on
the east and south; and by Cambodia and Laos on the
west.

The Major Administrative Divisions of South Vietnam are the
45 Provinces or "tinh."

The minor administrative divisions of South Vietnam are the
237 districts or "huyen."

	Provinces	Provincial Capitals
1.	Quang-Nam	Hoi-An
2.	Quang-Ngai	Quang-Ngai
3.	Quang-Tin	Tam-Ky
4.	Quang-Tri	Quang-Tri
5.	Thua-Thien	Hué
6.	Binh-Dinh	Quí-Nhon
7.	Binh-Thuan	Phan-Thiet
8.	Binh-Tuy	Ham-Tan
9.	Darlac	Banmethuot
10.	Lam-Dong	Bao-Loc
11.	Khanh-Hoa	Nha-Trang
12.	Kontum	Polei Krung
13.	Quang-Duc	Gia-Nghia
14.	Phu-Bon	Hau-Bon
15.	Phu-Yen	Tuy-Hoa
16.	Pleiku	Pleiku
17.	Ninh-Thuan	Phan-Rang
18.	Tuyen-Duc	Dalat
19.	Bien-Hoa	Bien-Hoa
20.	Binh-Duong	Phu-Cuong
21.	Binh-Long	An-Loc
22.	Hau-Nghia	Khien-Cuong
23.	Long-An	Tan-An
24.	Long-Khanh	Xuan-Loc
25.	Phuoc-Long	Phuoc-Binh
26.	Phuoc-Thanh	Phuoc-Vinh
27.	Phuoc-Tuy	Phuoc-Le
28.	Tay-Ninh	Tay-Ninh
29.	An-Giang	Long-Xuyen
30.	An-Xuyen	Quan-Long
31.	Ba-Xuyen	Khanh-Hung
32.	Bac-Lieu	Bac-Lieu

South Vietnam (continued)

33. Chau-Doc	Chau-Doc
34. Chuong-Thien	Vi-Thanh
35. Con-Son	Con-Son
36. Dinh-Tuong	My-Tho
37. Go-Cong	Go-Cong
38. Kien-Giang	Rach-Gia
39. Kien-Hoa	Truc-Giang
40. Kien-Phong	Cao-Lanh
41. Kien-Tuong	Moc-Hoa
42. Phong-Dinh	Can-Tho
43. Vinh-Binh	Phu-Vinh
44. Vinh-Long	Vinh-Long
45. Gia-Dinh	Gia-Dinh

Western Samoa (popular name)

The Independent State of Western Samoa (official name)

Apia (national capital)

Western Samoa is located in the South Pacific Ocean, in the area known as the Polynesian Island Group.

The Major Administrative Divisions of Western Samoa number 3:

1. The Municipality of Apia
2. The Local Council of Aleisa
3. The Administrative Office of Savaii Island

The minor administrative divisions may include the 44 territorial constituencies, but these are used only for legislative purposes.

Yemen (popular name)

The Arab Republic of Yemen (official name)

Sana (national capital)

Yemen is located in Southwestern Asia on the Arabian Peninsula. It is bounded by Saudi Arabia on the north; by Saudi Arabia and Aden on the east and south; and by the Red Sea on the west.

Yemen's Major Administrative Divisions are its 7 Provinces or "muhafazats."

Yemen's minor administrative divisions are called districts
or "qadas."

Provinces	Provincial Capitals
1. Sana	Sana
2. Ibb	Ibb
3. Taiz	Taiz
4. Hodeida	Hodeida
5. Hajjah	Hajjah
6. Saidah	Saidah
7. Radah	Radah

Yugoslavia (popular name)

The Socialist Federal Republic of Yugoslavia (official name)

"Federnativan Norodna Republika Jugoslavija" (native name)

Belgrade (capital city)

Yugoslavia is located in Eastern Europe. It is bounded by
Austria, Hungary, and Rumania on the north; by Hungary,
Rumania, and Bulgaria on the east; by Greece and Al-
bania on the south; and by Albania, the Adriatic Sea, and
Italy on the west.

The Major Administrative Divisions of Yugoslavia comprise
6 people's republics and 2 autonomous Serb divisions.

The minor administrative divisions include 75 districts
("srezovi") and 566 communes ("postine.")

Pepple's Republics	Administrative Seats
1. Bosna i Hercegovina	Sarajevo
2. Hrvatska (Croatia)	Zagreb
3. Makedvnija (Macedonia)	Skopje
4. Crna Gora (Montenegro)	Titograd
5. Slovinija (Slovenia)	Ljubljana
6. Srbija (Serbia)	Belgrade

Note: Under administration of Serbia are 2 autonomous divisions:
1. The Kosovo Metohija Auto. Region   Pristina
2. The Vojvodina Auto. Province   Novi Sad

Zambia (popular name)

The Republic of Zambia (official name)

Lusaka (capital city)

Zambia is located in South-central Africa. It is bounded by
Congo (Léopoldville) and Tanzania on the north; by Malawi and Mozambique on the east; by Rhodesia and Bechuanaland on the south; and by South-West Africa and Angola on the west.

The Major Administrative Divisions of Zambia number 8
and are called provinces.

The minor administrative divisions are the 52 districts and
36 local authorities.

Provinces	Provincial Capitals
1. Western	Ndola
2. Luapula	Fort Rosebery
3. Northern	Kasama
4. Central	Broken Hill
5. Eastern	Fort Jameson
6. Southern	Livingstone
7. North-Western	Solwezi
8. Barotseland	Mongu

Index

Arussi, 45
Arvai-Khar, 87
Asan, 144
Ascalon, 67
Ascoli Piceno, 69
Aselle, 45
Ashkhabad, 130
Ash Shamaliyah, 118
Ashanti, 54
Ashburton, 91
Ashhurst, 92
Ashley, 91
Ashmore and Cartier Is., 13
Asir, 110
Asmara, 45
Assaba, 84
Assam, 62
Assen, 90
Asti, 69
Asunción, 100
Asyut, 133
Atacama, 29
Atakpamé, 124
Atar, 85
Athens, 54
Athiémé, 41
Ati, 28
Atjeh, 63
Atlahoué, 41
Atlanta, 142
Atlántico, 34
Atlantida, 59
Attiki, 55
Attopeu, 77
Au-Baroastrandar, 61
Aube, 47
Auch, 47
Auck, 91
Auckland, 92
Aude, 47
Audhali, 114
Augusta, 143
Au-Húnavatns, 61
Aurillac, 47
Au-Skaftafells, 61
Aust-Agder, 97
Austral Islands, 49
Austin, 143

Australia, 12
Australian Antarctic, 13
Australian Capital, 13
Austria, 14
Auxerre, 49
Aveiro, 105
Avelino, 69
Aveyron, 47
Avignon, 49
Avila, 116
Awabil, 115
Awatere, 91
Ayacucho, 101
Aydin, 128
Aylesbury, 134
Ayion Oros, 55
Ayr, 138
Ayre, 139
Aysén, 29
Azad Kashmir, 99
Azerbaijan S.S.R., 130
Azogues, 44
Azua, 43
Azua de Compostella, 43
Azuay, 44
'Azzan, 114

Baabda, 77
Babahoyo, 44
Baboua, 25
Bacau, 108
Bac Can, 152
Bac-Lieu, 153
Bacolod, 103
Bács-Kiskum, 60
Badajoz, 116
Badakhshán, 9
Baden-Württemburg, 53
Badulla, 27
Baerhum, 97
Bafang, 23
Bafatá, 106
Baghdad, 65
Baghlan, 9
Baglung, 89
Bagmati, 89
Bahama Islands, 139
Bahawalpur, 99

Bahia, 18
Bahrain, 15
Bahr el Ghazel, 118
Baia-Mare, 108
Baibokoum, 28
Baidoa, 113
Baie du Levrier, 85
Baihan, 115
Bairiki, 139
Baixo Alentejo, 105
Baja California, 85
Baja California Sur, 86
Bajagós, 106
Baja Verapaz, 56
Bakala, 26
Bakouma, 26
Baku, 130
Bakwanga, 37
Balanga, 102
Balboa, 144
Balboa Heights, 143
Balclutha, 91
Bale, 45
Baleares, 117
Balhaf, 114
Bali, 64
Balikesir, 128
Balqa, 73
Baluchistan, 65
Balzers, 79
Bamako, 83
Bambari, 25
Bamboutos, 23
Bamenda, 23
Bamoun, 23
Banat, 108
Bandjarmasin, 64
Bandung, 64
Banekoura, 41
Banff, 138
Bangalore, 62
Bangangté, 23
Bangassou, 25
Bangkok, 122
Bangued, 102
Bangui, 25
Banī, 43
Banmethuot, 153

Banská Bystrica, 40
Bao-Loc, 153
Baoruco, 43
Barahona, 43
Baranya, 60
Barbados, 139
Barcelona, 116
Barceloneta, 146
Bari, 68
Barinas, 151
Bar-le-Duc, 48
Barnsley, 137
Barotseland, 156
Barqah, 78
Barquisimeto, 151
Barranquillo, 34
Barranquitos, 147
Barrigada, 144
Barrow-In-Furness, 135
Barun-Urt, 87
Basco, 102
Basel, 120
Basel Land, 120
Basel Stadt, 120
Bashkirian A.R., 130
Basilicata, 68
Basra, 65
Bas-Rhin, 48
Bassac, 77
Bassangoa, 25
Bassari, 124
Basse, 52
Bassein, 20
Basse-Kotto, 25
Basses-Alps, 47
Basses-Pyrénées, 48
Basse-Terre, 49
Basseterre, 139
Basso Juba, 113
Basutoland, 139
Bata, 117
Bataan, 102
Batangafo, 26
Batangas, 102
Batanes, 102
Bath, 135
Batha, 28
Bathurst, 51
161

Batinah, 88
Batna, 11
Baton Rouge, 143
Batouri, 23
Battambang, 22
Batticaloa, 27
Batumi, 131
Bauchi, 97
Ba-Xuyen, 153
Bayamon, 146
Bayan-Khongor, 87
Bayan-Uleggi, 87
Bayern, 53
Bay of Islands, 91
Bayombong, 102
Beauvais, 48
Bécéscsaba, 60
Bechuanaland, 139
Bedford, 134
Bedfordshire, 134
Beersheba, 67
Begemder, 45
Behera, 133
Beira, 107
Beira Alta, 105
Beira Baixa, 105
Beira Litoral, 105
Beirut, 77
Beja (Portugal), 105
Beja (Tunisia), 127
Békés, 60
Belait, 19
Belem, 18
Belet Wein, 113
Belfort, 49
Belgium, 15
Belgrade, 155
Belize, 139
Bellinzonna, 120
Belluno, 69
Belo Horizonte, 18
Bembéréké, 41
Benguela, 106
Benha, 133
Beni, 17
Benin, 97
Beni Suef, 133
Bénoué, 23

Benue, 97
Berat, 10
Berbérati, 25
Berbice, 140
Bergamo, 69
Bergen, 98
Berkshire, 134
Berlarati, 26
Benadir, 113
Bender Kassim, 113
Benefactor, 43
Benevento, 69
Benghazi, 78
Bermuda, 139
Berne, 119
Berry Islands, 14
Berwick, 138
Besançon, 47
Beverly, 135
Beyla, 57
Bhairawa, 89
Bheri, 89
Bhimphedi, 89
Bhopal, 62
Bhubaneswar, 63
Bhutan, 16
Bialystock, 104
Bié-Cuando Cubango, 106
Bien-Hoa, 153
Bihar, 62
Bilboa, 117
Bilecik, 128
Bilma, 95
Biltine, 28
Bimbo, 25
Bimini Islands, 141
Bingol, 128
Binh-Dinh, 153
Binh-Duong, 153
Binh-Long, 153
Bingh-Thuan, 153
Binh-Tuy, 153
Bio-Bio, 29
Bi'r Ahmad, 115
Bir'Ali, 115
Birao, 25
Biratnagar, 89
Birkenhead, 135

Boyacá, 34
Bozoum, 25
Brabant, 16
Bradford, 136
Braga, 105
Bragança, 105
Brakna, 85
Brasilia, 17
Brasov, 108
Bratislava, 40
Brazil, 17
Brazzaville, 35
Brecknock, 137
Brecon, 137
Bremen, 53
Bremerdorp, 140
Brescia, 69
Bria, 25
Bridgetown, 139
Brighton, 136
Brikama, 52
Brindisi, 69
Brisbane, 13
Bristol, 136
Bristol Bay, 146
British Antarctic, 139
Britich Columbia, 24
British Guiana, 139
British Honduras, 139
British Solomon Islands, 139
British Virgin Islands, 139
Brno, 40
Broken Hill, 156
Brong Ahofo, 54
Bruce, 91
Bruges, 16
Brunei, 18
Brunei and Muara, 19
Brunei Town, 18
Brussels, 16
Buar-Baboua, 25
Bubanza, 21
Bubaque, 106
Bucaramanga, 35
Buchanan, 78
Bucharest, 108
Buckinghamshire, 134

Budapest, 60
Búdardalur, 61
Buenos Aires, 12
Buganda, 132
Bugisu, 132
Bujumbura, 21
Bukavu, 37
Bukedi, 132
Bukidon, 103
Bukit Panjang, 113
Bukittinggi, 63
Bukoba, 122
Bulacan, 102
Bulawayo, 108
Bulgan, 87
Bulgaria, 19
Buller, 91
Bulnes, 31
Bungoma, 74
Bunia, 37
Bunyoro, 132
Burao, 113
Burdur, 128
Burgenland, 15
Burgos, 116
Buriram, 123
Burma, 20
Burnley, 136
Bursa, 128
Burton-On-Trent, 136
Burundi, 21
Bururi, 21
Bury, 136
Buryat A.R., 130
Bury St. Edmunds, 135
Bu'si, 115
Buskerud, 97
Busoga, 132
Butare, 109
Bute, 138
Butha-Buthe, 141
Butuan, 103
Byakar, 16
Bydgoszcz, 104
Byelorussian S.S.R., 130
Byumba, 109

Caaguazú, 100
Caapucú, 100
Caazapá, 100
Cabañas, 45
Cabinda, 106
Cabo Delgado, 107
Cabo Gracias a Dios, 95
Cabo Rojo, 147
Cáceres, 117
Cachapoal, 31
Cacheu, 106
Cádiz, 116
Caen, 47
Caernarvon, 137
Cagayan, 102
Cagayan de Oro, 103
Cagliari, 68
Caguas, 147
Cahors, 48
Cairo, 133
Caithness, 138
Cajamarca, 101
Calabria, 68
Calapan, 102
Calavi, 40
Calbuco, 32
Calcutta, 63
Caldas, 34
Cali, 35
California, 142
Callao, 101
Caltanissetta, 69
Calvados, 47
Camagüey, 38
Camarines Norte, 102
Camarines Sur, 102
Cambodia, 21
Cambridge, 134
Cambridgeshire, 134
Cameroon, 22
Campania, 68
Campeche, 85
Campobasso, 69
Camuy, 146
Canada, 23
Canakkale, 128
Cañar, 44

Canberra, 12
Candia, 55
Canelones, 149
Cañet, 31
Canillo, 11
Cankiri, 128
Cantal, 47
Canterbury, 136
Can-Tho, 154
Canton Island, 139
Canton And Enderbury Is. , 139
Cao-Bang, 152
Cap Bon, 127
Cape, 114
Cape Coast, 54
Capellen, 79
Cape Mount, 78
Capetown, 114
Cape Verde Islands, 105
Cap-Haitien, 58
Cap-Vert, 111
Caquetá, 35
Carabobo, 151
Caracas, 150
Carazo, 94
Carcassonne, 47
Carchi, 44
Cardiff, 137
Cardigan, 137
Carlisle, 134
Carlow, 66
Carmachs-Kluane, 25
Carmarthen, 137
Carmona, 106
Carnot, 26
Carolina, 146
Caroline Island, 148
Caroni, 125
Carrick-On-Shannon, 66
Carson City, 143
Cartagena, 34
Cartago, 38
Carterton, 93
Casablanca, 88
Cassamance, 111
Castela Branco, 105
Castellón, 117

167

Comayagua, 59
Combarbalá, 30
Comb-Béchar, 11
Comerioq, 147
Commewijne, 90
Como, 69
Comoro Archipelago, 48
Conakry, 57
Concepción (Chile), 29
Concepción (Paraguay), 100
Concord, 143
Congo (Brazzaville), 35
Congo-Central, 37
Congo (Léopoldville), 36
Connecticut, 142
Con-Son, 154
Constanta, 108
Constantine, 11
Constitución, 31
Cook, 91
Copán, 59
Copenhagen, 41
Copiapó, 29
Coquillatville, 37
Coquimbo, 29
Cordoba (Argentina), 12
Cordoba (Colombia), 35
Córdoba (Spain), 116
Corfu, 56
Cork, 66
Corn Islands, 148
Cornwall, 134
Coro, 151
Coromandel, 91
Coronel, 31
Coronel Oviedo, 100
Coronie, 90
Corozal (Br. Honduras), 140
Corozal (Puerto Rico), 146
Corrèze, 47
Corrientes, 12
Corse, 47
Cortés, 59
Corum, 128
Cosenza, 69
Costa Rica, 37
Cotabato, 103
Côte-D'Or, 49

Côte-du-Nord, 47
Côte Française des Somalie, 49
Cotonou, 40
Cotopaxi, 44
Cottbus, 52
Couquenes, 30
Coutances, 48
Coventry, 136
Craiova, 109
Cremona, 69
Creuse, 47
Crisana, 108
Cristobal, 144
Crna Gora, 155
Croatia, 155
Croydon, 136
Csongrád, 60
Cuanza Norte, 106
Cuanza Sul, 106
Cuba, 38
Cucuta, 35
Cuena, 116
Cuenca, 44
Cueravaca, 86
Cuilapa, 57
Culiacan, 86
Culverden, 91
Cumaná, 151
Cumberland, 134
Cundinamarca, 35
Cuneo, 69
Cupar, 138
Curaçao, 90
Curacautin, 31
Curepto, 31
Curicó, 29
Curitiba, 18
Cuscatlán, 45
Cusco, 101
Cuvette-Central, 37
Cyangugu, 109
Cyprus, 39
Czechoslovakia, 39

Dabola, 58
Dacca, 99
Dadra and Nagar Haveli, 63

168

Djougou, 41
Dnor, 29
Doala, 71
Doba, 28
Dobrogea, 108
Dodoma, 121
Dogondoutchi, 95
Doha, 107
Dolgellau, 137
Dolisie, 36
Domagnano, 110
Dominica, 139
Dominican Republic, 42
Doncaster, 136
Donegal, 66
Dorado, 146
Dorchester, 135
Dordogne, 47
Dorsetshire, 135
Dosso, 95
Douala, 23
Doubs, 47
Douglas, 139
Douro Litoral, 105
Dover, 142
Dowa, 81
Down, 138
Downpatrick, 138
Draguignan, 48
Drama, 55
Drammen, 97
Drente, 90
Dresden, 52
Drôme, 47
Dschang, 23
Duarte, 43
Dubai, 126
Dublin, 66
Dubréka, 58
Dudinka, 131
Dudley, 136
Dukye, 16
Dumaguete, 103
Dumfries, 138
Dunbarton, 138
Dundalk, 66
Dundee, 138
Dunedin, 93

Dungarvan, 66
Duns, 138
Durango, 85
Durazno, 149
Durham, 135
Durrës, 10
Dushanbe, 130
Düsseldorf, 53
Duvauchelle, 91
Dzabkhan, 87
Dzaoudzi, 50

East Berlin, 52
Eastbourne, 136
East Central, 14
Eastern (Ceylon), 27
Eastern (Ghana), 54
Eastern (Ivory Coast), 71
Eastern (Kenya), 74
Eastern (Saudi Arabia), 110
Eastern (Sierra Leone), 111
Eastern (Uganda), 132
Eastern (Zambia), 156
Eastern Azerbaijan, 64
Eastern Flevoland, 90
Eastern Highlands, 14
Eastern Nigeria, 97
Eastern Tahsil, 112
Eastern Tutuila, 145
East Gobi, 87
East Ham, 136
East Java, 64
East Kalimantan, 64
East Lothian, 138
East Mengo, 132
East Nusa-Tenggara, 64
East Pakistan, 98
East Suffolk, 135
East Sussex, 135
Ebolowa, 23
Echternach, 80
Ecuador, 43
Edessa, 56
Edinburgh, 138
Edirne, 128
Edmonton, 24
Eger, 60
Egmont, 91

175

184

Maikop, 131
Maimana, 9
Mai-Ndombe, 37
Maine (Niger), 96
Maine, (U. S. A.), 143
Maine-et-Loire, 48
Maine Soroa, 96
Maintirano, 81
Mainz, 53
Maipu, 30
Majunga, 80
Majuro, 144
Makale, 45
Makani, 112
Makassar, 64
Makedvnija, 155
Makeni, 111
Makokou, 51
Makoua, 36
Makung, 34
Malacca, 82
Málaga, 116
Malagasy, 80
Malakal, 118
Malaku, 64
Malanje, 106
Malanville, 41
Malatya, 128
Malawi, 81
Malaybalay, 103
Malaysia, 82
Malcolm, 83
Malden Island, 148
Maldive Islands, 83
Maldonado, 150
Malé, 83
Mali (Guinea), 58
Mali (Mali), 83
Malleco, 30
Malmo, 119
Malmøhus, 119
Malolas, 102
Malta, 84
Maltese Central, 84
Malvern, 92
Mamfe, 23
Mamou, 58
Man, 71

Manabi, 44
Managua, 94
Manahiki Island, 148
Manaia, 93
Manama, 15
Mananjary, 80
Manati, 147
Manaus, 18
Manawatu, 92
Manche, 48
Manchester (Jamaica), 71
Manchester (U. K.), 136
Mandalay, 20
Mandal-Gobi, 87
Mandeville, 71
Mango, 124
Mangonui, 92
Manica e Sofala, 107
Manicaland, 108
Maniema, 37
Maniototo, 92
Manipur, 63
Manisa, 129
Manitoba, 24
Manizales, 34
Mankaiana, 141
Mannar, 27
Mansa Konko, 52
Mansôa, 106
Mansura, 133
Mantova, 69
Manu'a, 145
Manukau, 92
Manus, 14
Mao, 28
Mara, 121
Maracaibo, 151
Maracay, 151
Maradi, 95
Maramures, 108
Maranhao, 18
Maras, 129
March, 134
Mardin, 129
Margui-Wandala, 23
Mari A. R., 130
Maribo, 42
Maricao, 147

Mariestad, 119
Marinduque, 102
Marioneth, 137
Marlborough, 92
Marne, 48
Maroni, 49
Maroua, 23
Marowijne, 90
Marquesas Islands, 49
Marrakech, 88
Marseille, 47
Marshall Islands, 144
Martinborough, 91
Martinique, 49
Marton, 92
Maryland (Liberia), 78
Maryland (U. S. A.), 143
Masaka, 132
Masaya, 94
Masbate, 103
Maseru, 139
Massachusetts, 143
Massakory, 28
Massana, 11
Massenya, 28
Massin, 103
Masterton, 92
Matagalpa, 95
Matakaoa, 92
Matale, 27
Matamata, 92
Matameye, 96
Matanuska-Susitna, 146
Matanzas, 38
Mataquito, 31
Matara, 27
Mataram, 64
Mata-Uto, 49
Matera, 69
Matlock, 134
Matsue, 72
Matsuyama, 73
Matto Grasso, 18
Maturin, 151
Maule, 30
Maullín, 32
Maun, 140
Maunabo, 146

Mauputasi, 145
Mauriceville, 92
Mauritania, 84
Mauritius, 139
Mausatta, 115
Mavren, 79
Mayaguana, 141
Mayaguez, 147
Mayahi, 96
Mayaro, 125
Mayo (Canada), 25
Mayo (Ireland), 66
Mayo-Danai, 23
Mayo-Kebbi, 28
May Pen, 71
Mayenne, 48
Mayumba, 51
Mazandaran, 64
Mazár-i-Sharif, 9
Mazatenango, 57
Mbabane, 139
M'Baiki, 25
Mbale, 132
Mbalmayo, 23
Mbarara, 132
Mbeya, 122
M'Bigou, 51
M'Bomou, 25
Mbouda, 23
McDonald and Heard Is., 13
Mchinji, 82
Meath, 66
Mecca, 110
Mechi, 89
Medan, 63
Medea, 11
Medellin, 34
Medenine, 127
Medouneu, 51
Mefou, 23
Mekambo, 51
Meknes, 88
Melfi, 29
Melbourne, 13
Melilla, 117
Melipilla, 30
Melo, 149
Melun, 48

Mombassa, 74
Monaco, 86
Monaco City, 86
Monaco-Ville, 86
Monagas, 151
Monaghan, 66
Monaragala, 27
Mondolkiri, 22
Mongo, 28
Mongolia, 86Mongoumba, 26
Mongu, 156
Monmouth, 137
Monrovia, 77
Mons, 16
Montana, 143
Montauban, 48
Mont-de-Marsan, 48
Monte Carlo, 86
Monte Cristi, 43
Montegiardino, 110
Montego Bay, 71
Montenegro, 155
Monteria, 35
Monterrey, 86
Montevideo, 149
Montgomery (U. K.), 137
Montgomery (U. S. A.), 142
Montpelier, 143
Montpellier, 47
Montserrado, 78
Montserrat, 139
Mopti, 84
Moquegua, 101
Morant Bay, 71
Morazán, 45
Morbihan, 48
Mordovian A. R. , 130
Morelas, 86
Morelia, 85
Möre og Romsdal, 98
Morioka, 73
Moriscal, 100
Morobe, 14
Morocco, 87
Morogoro, 121
Morondava, 81
Moroto, 132
Morovis, 147

Moscow, 129
Moselle, 48
Mosgiel, 93
Moshi, 121
Mosquito Coast, 59
Moss, 98
Mossaka, 36
Mossendjo, 36
Mostaganem, 11
Mosul, 65
Movila, 51
Moulins, 47
Moulmein, 20
Moundou, 28
Moundou Centre Urbain, 28
Mountain, 102
Mount Herbert, 92
Mount Libanus, 77
Moussoro, 28
Mouyondzi, 36
Moxico, 106
Moyamba, 112
Moyen-Chari, 28
Moyen-Congo, 37
Moyen-Ogooué, 51
Moyo, 133
Moyobamba, 101
Mozambique, 105
Mtwara, 121
Mubende, 132
Mudiyah, 114
Mudug, 113
Mugla, 129
Muharraq, 15
Muhinga, 21
Múla, 61
Mulaku, 83
Mulchen, 31
Mullingar, 66
Multan, 99
Mungo, 23
Munich, 53
Muong May, 77
Muramvya, 21
Murchison, 92
Murcia, 117
Mures Autonoma Maghiara,
108

Murun, 87
Mus, 129
Musaymir, 115
Muscat and Oman, 88
Muscat and Matrah, 88
Muscat City, 88
Mutsamudu, 50
Muzaffarabad, 99
M'Vouti, 36
Mwanza, 121
Myitkyina, 21
Mýrar, 61
Mysore, 62
My-Tho, 154
Mytilene, 55
Mzimba, 81

Naas, 66
Nablus, 73
Nacoame, 59
Naga, 102
Nagaland, 63
Nagano, 73
Nagasaki, 72
Nagorny Karabakh, 131
Nagoya, 73
Naguabo, 147
Naha, 144
Nairiyah, 65
Nairn, 138
Nairobi, 74
Nakhichevan, 131
Nakhornnayok, 123
Nakhornpathom, 122
Nakhornphanom, 123
Nakhornratchsima, 123
Nakhornsawan, 124
Nakhornsrithamrat, 123
Naknek, 146
Nakuru, 74
Nalchik, 130
Nam Dinh, 152
Namp'o, 75
Nampula, 107
Nam Tha, 76
Namur, 16
Nan, 124
Nanchang, 33

Nancy, 48
Nanga-Eboko, 23
Nangarhar, 9
Nanking, 33
Nanning, 33
Nantes, 48
Nantou, 34
Napier, 92
Naples, 68
Napo, 44
Napoli, 68
Nara, 72
Naranjito, 147
Nara-Thiwat, 123
Narayani, 89
Nariño, 35
Nariva, 125
Naryan-Mar, 131
Nashville, 143
Nassau, 139
Natal, 114
Natitingou, 40
Nauplia, 55
Nauru, 13
Navarra, 117
Navassa Island, 148
Nayarit, 86
Ncheu, 81
Ndé, 23
N'Dele, 25
N'Dendé, 51
N'Djole, 51
Ndola, 156
Nebraska, 143
Neembucu, 100
Negri Sembilan, 82
Negros Occidental, 103
Negros Oriental, 103
Neiafu, 125
Neiba, 43
Neiva, 35
Nejd, 110
N'Eliya, 27
Nelson, 93
Nema, 85
Nenagh, 66
Nenets, 131
Nepal, 89

Quang Binh, 152
Quang-Duc, 153
Quang-Nam, 153
Quang-Ngai, 153
Quang-Ninh, 152
Quang-Tin, 153
Quang-Tri, 153
Quan-Long, 153
Quaretaro, 86
Quargla, 11
Quebec, 24
Quebradillas, 148
Queensland, 13
Queenstown, 92
Quelimane, 107
Quemoy, 34
Quetta, 99
Quezaltenango, 57
Quezon, 102
Quezon City, 102
Quibdó, 34
Quillota, 30
Quimper, 47
Quinchao, 32
Qui-Nhon, 153
Quintano Roo, 86
Quito, 43
Quito Sueño Bank, 148
Quthing, 141

Rabat, 87
Rabaul, 14
Rach-Gia, 154
Radah, 155
Radnor, 137
Raetihi, 93
Rafai, 26
Ragged Island and Cays, 141
Raglan, 92
Ragusa, 70
Raiatéa Island, 49
Rajasthan, 63
Rajbiraj, 89
Rajshani, 99
Raleigh, 143
Ramadi, 65
Ramlat al-Hamra, 126
Ramle, 67

Rancagua, 30
Randers, 42
Ranfurly, 92
Rangárvalla, 61
Rangiokei, 92
Rangiora, 92
Rangiroa, 49
Rangoon, 20
Ranong, 123
Rapati, 89
Raqqa, 121
Ras al Khaimah, 126
Ratanakiri, 22
Ratburi, 122
Ratnapura, 27
Ravenna, 70
Rawalpindi, 98
Rawene, 92
Rawson, 12
Rayong, 123
Razrad, 20
Reading, 134
Recife, 18
Rédange, 80
Reefton, 92
Reggio Calabria, 68
Reggio di Calabria, 70
Reggio nell'Emilia, 70
Regina, 24
Rehvat, 67
Remich, 80
Renfrew, 138
Rennes, 47
Resht, 64
Resistencia, 12
Retalhuleu, 57
Rethymnon, 56
Reykjavik, 61
Rezaiyeh, 64
Rheinland-Pfalz, 53
Rhode Island, 143
Rhodes, 55
Rhodesia, 107
Rhône, 48
Riauw, 63
Ribatejo, 105
Ribe, 42
Richmond, 143

San Felipe (Chile), 29
San Felipe (Colombia), 35
San Felipe (Venezuela), 151
San Fernando (Chile), 29
San Fernando (Philippines), 102
San Fernando (Trinidad), 126
San Fernando (Venezuela), 151
San Francisco de Macorís, 43
San Francisco Gotera, 45
San German, 147
Sangha, 36
San Giovanni, 110
Sangmélima, 23
Sangre Grande, 125
Saniquellie, 78
San José (Costa Rica), 38
San José (Uruguay), 150
San José de Buenavista, 103
San Juan (Argentina), 12
San Juan (Dominican Republic), 43
San Juan (Puerto Rico), 143
San Juan Bautista, 100
San Juan de los Morros, 151
Sankuru, 37
San Lorenzo, 147
San Luis, 12
San Luis Potosi, 86
San Marcos, 57
San Marino, 109
San Martín, 101
San Miguel, 45
Sannandaj, 65
San Pedro, 100
San Pedro de Macorís, 43
San Pedro Sula, 59
San Rafael, 43
San Salvador (El Salvador), 44
San Salvador (Bahamas), 141
San Sebastian (Spain), 117
San Sebastian (Puerto Rico), 148
Sansonate, 45
Santa Ana, 45

Santa Bárbara, 59
Santa Catarina, 18
Santa Clara, 38
Santa Cruz (Argentina), 12
Santa Cruz (Bolivia), 17
Santa Cruz (Chile), 31
Santa Cruz (Philippines), 102
Santa Cruz de Barahona, 43
Santa Cruz del Quiché, 56
Santa Cruz de Tenerife, 117
Santa Fe (Argentina), 12
Santa Fe (U. S. A.), 143
Santa Isabel (Spain), 117
Santa Isabel (Puerto Rico), 147
Santa Marta, 35
Santander (Colombia), 35
Santander (Spain), 116
Santarém (Portugal), 105
Santa Rosa (Argentina), 12
Santa Rosa (Guatemala), 57
Santa Rosa de Copán, 59
Santiago (Chile), 29
Santiago (Dominican Republic), 43
Santiago (Paraguay), 100
Santiago de Cuba, 39
Santiago del Estero, 12
Santiago de los Caballeros, 43
Santiago Morona, 44
Santiago Rodriguez, 43
Sant Julia de Loria, 11
Santo Domingo, 42
San Vicente (Chile), 31
San Vicente (El Salvador), 45
São Domingos, 106
Saole, 145
Saône-et-Loire, 48
São Paulo, 18
São Salvador, 106
São Tomé, 106
São Tomé e Principe, 106
Saoura, 11
Sapporo, 73
Saraburi, 123
Sarajevo, 155
Saramacca, 90
Sarask, 130
Saravane, 77

200

Tulle, 47
Tumbes, 101
Tunapuna, 125
Tunceli, 129
Tungurahua, 44
Tunis, 127
Tunisia, 127
Tunja, 34
Tura, 131
Turin, 68
Turkey, 127
Turkmen S. S. R., 130
Turku, 46
Turnovo, 19
Turunja-Porin, 46
Tutong, 19
Tuxtla Gutierrez, 85

Uawa, 93
Ubangi, 37
Ubonratch-thani, 123
Ubsa-Nor, 87
Ubur-Khangai, 87
Udmart, 131
Udornthani, 123
Uéle, 37
Ufa, 130
Ufra, 129
Uganda, 132
Uige, 106
Ukrainian S. S. R., 130
Ulan Bator, 86
Ulan-Gom, 87
Ulan-Ude, 130
Ulgi, 87
Ultima Esperanza, 32
Umatac, 144
Umbria, 68
Umea, 119
Umtali, 108
Undurkhan, 87
Union Islands, 148
(Union of Soviet Socialist
Republics) U. S. S. R., 129
United Arab Republic, 133
United Kingdom, 134
United States, 142
Unité-Kasaienne, 37

Uodenmaan, 46
Upper, 54
Upper Aulaqi, 115
Upper Nile, 118
Upper River, 52
Upper Volta, 149
Upper Yafa, 115
Uppsala, 119
Uri, 120
Uruguay, 149
Usak, 129
Ushuaia, 12
Usti-nad Laben, 40
Ust-Orda-Buryat, 131
Ust-Ordynsky, 131
Usulatán, 45
Utah, 143
Uthai-thani, 124
Utorua, 49
Utrecht, 90
Utsunomiya, 72
Uttaradit, 124
Uttar Pradesh, 63
Utuado, 147
Uva, 27
Uzbek S. S. R., 130

Vaasan, 46
Vadsø, 97
Vaduz, 79
Vaifanua, 145
Vakinankaratra à Antsirabé,
80
Valais, 120
Valdivia, 30
Valée du Fleuve, 111
Valence, 47
Valencia (Spain), 117
Valencia (Venezuela), 151
Valladolid, 116
Valle, 59
Valle D'Aosta, 68
Valle del Cauca, 35
Valparaiso, 30
Valverde, 43
Van, 129
Vanersborg, 119
Vannes, 48